Praise for Dragons to Butterflies

"All I can say right now ... is WOW.
I never dreamed there was another soul that lived with such similar torment ... yet I have come to learn that sometimes the clowns are the saddest most traumatized souls and they will go to any length to protect anyone from finding out the 'truth'. Kudos to you, Johnnie and here's to the slaying of the dragons"

Debbie Morris

"You have a strong voice Johnnie, and an important story to tell. Tell your story"

Chip St. Clair,
New York Times Best Selling Author
of "The Butterfly Garden"

"F. Scott Fitzgerald said, 'Show me a hero and I'll show you a tragedy'. *Dragons to Butterflies* takes you on a journey of tragedy to triumph, from the broken heart of an abused child to the beautiful soul of a man."

Suzi Wright Henry

OTHER TITLES BY JOHNNIE CALLOWAY

Taming the Dragon, 1991

DRAGONS **to** BUTTERFLIES

THE METAMORPHOSIS OF A MAN

Little Sister Linda,
you are appreciated
more than you know

JOHNNIE CALLOWAY

BALBOA
PRESS

A DIVISION OF HAY HOUSE

Balboa Press books may be ordered through booksellers or by contacting:

Balboa Press
A Division of Hay House
1663 Liberty Drive
Bloomington, IN 47403
www.balboapress.com
1 (877) 407-4847

Because of the dynamic nature of the Internet, any web addresses or
links contained in this book may have changed since publication and
may no longer be valid. The views expressed in this work are solely those
of the author and do not necessarily reflect the views of the publisher,
and the publisher hereby disclaims any responsibility for them.

The author of this book does not dispense medical advice or prescribe the use
of any technique as a form of treatment for physical, emotional, or medical
problems without the advice of a physician, either directly or indirectly. The
intent of the author is only to offer information of a general nature to help
you in your quest for emotional and spiritual well-being. In the event you use
any of the information in this book for yourself, which is your constitutional
right, the author and the publisher assume no responsibility for your actions.

Any people depicted in stock imagery provided by Thinkstock are
models, and such images are being used for illustrative purposes only.
Certain stock imagery © Thinkstock.

Print information available on the last page.

ISBN: 978-1-5043-5410-3 (sc)
ISBN: 978-1-5043-5412-7 (hc)
ISBN: 978-1-5043-5411-0 (e)

Library of Congress Control Number: 2016904984

Balboa Press rev. date: 3/29/2016

CONTENTS

DEDICATION

Dragons to Butterflies is written in dedication to my dad for all that he taught me about the durability of the human heart. His teachings did not come in the traditional sense. Most of what he taught has taken a lifetime for me to understand. I believe that he and I made a pact, perhaps many lifetimes ago, that he would help me learn forgiveness of what most would deem as unforgivable circumstances.

First, he taught me about hatred in all its glory but in the end he taught me about forgiveness and love, and became my friend. To him I am very grateful for playing such a tremendous role in my becoming the man I am today.

Perhaps if you stay with *Dragons to Butterflies* through to its end, you will see how the ogre of my youth became the reigning angel of my life.

With much love,

Johnnie Calloway

PREFACE

Through most of my adult life I have been told, "You should write a book." Why? I lived through seizures in my infancy; the loss of my mom at the age of five; rage, sexual confusion and the violence of an alcoholic father; anger at God and my own alcoholism and drug addiction and multiple mental illness diagnosis'.

My desire to overcome and rise above has led me to many spiritual teachings that have in turn, led me to the forgiveness of those I felt had harmed me, of myself (at least to some degree) and most of all of God.

In 1991 as a result of being encouraged to write the first time, I wrote and published *Taming the Dragon,* a metaphor of my life (I was not ready to disclose the whole truth). I put that book to bed and pretty much forgot it and, along with it, put to sleep my dreams of helping others, which had been its intention.

Then in January of 2015, through a series of *coincidental* meetings I once again was told to write. I do not know why, but I never questioned it. I just grabbed my computer and started typing. Once I began I simply could not stop ... the writing took on a life all its own. Nine weeks and 22 chapters later birth had been given to *Dragons to Butterflies.* I believe with all of my heart that my entire life has been lived for the words that came pouring out of me onto these pages.

My greatest hope is that some will find solace in these writings, and learn that they can endure and that they are not alone.

ACKNOWLEDGEMENTS

There are so many people to whom I am so grateful. I would seriously have to write another book to list them all. My heart sings with gratitude for all those who have assisted me in my walk back out of the woods.

The first has got to be my mom. In the early years of my recovery one of my many therapists asked me, "Do you know what got you through all the insanity that you have lived through?" My answer was, "Good luck?" She then told me, "Your mother loved you enough in those short five years she had with you to get you through all the rest." And I knew it was so.

My dad … many have asked, "How can you be grateful for a man that put you through so much hell?" I cannot explain that here. Hopefully *Dragons to Butterflies* will. I always loved him and I know today that a large part of the torment he lived was in loving his children and not being able to show it or to really feel it. I am grateful to and for him.

My beautiful sisters: Jackie (we shared the same mother and father), Marsha (same father) and Jane Ann (same mother). Each of them have played major roles in my life and have tried the best they could to love me and be there for me in my hour(s) of need. I am forever grateful for the part each has played in my life.

The many friends' mothers who did the best they could to be a mother figure for me in my very troubled childhood. And all the older women who still try to mother me today (Barbara).

To all the men that tried to teach me how to be a man and to have some kind of work ethic. Gerald W. taught me to take pride in what I do or not to do it.

The state reformatory Boys Camp gave me a taste of respect for myself, for others, and for authority. To this establishment I will be forever grateful.

To all the Twelve Step fellowships I have had the honor and privilege to be a part of and the men and women within those rooms.

To 'A Course in Miracles' for all it has taught me about an unconditionally loving God.

The many mentors who were delivered to me at just the right time and in just the right circumstance to teach me whatever was next for me to learn.

In order of appearance: Ed Cooper my mentor, my friend and my brother. None of what I am today would be real for me without Ed. He trusted me when I was untrustworthy and therefore taught me how to trust. He guided me when I was lost, taught me to laugh in the presence of my own tears and he helped me to become a man. So much of who I am today is a result of Ed being there for me in the beginning.

Callie Chappell Nicholas was my first A Course in Miracles teacher and my therapist off and on for many years. She still is a great support today. Callie has given me more tools for self-love and understanding than I can even remember. She has always guided me in the direction of self-forgiveness and forgiveness of others. It was Callie teaching me the importance of forgiving that led me to forgiving my father which is the reason for *Dragons to Butterflies*. We can all be grateful there is a Callie in this world.

Gerald Howell with his simplistic and practical wisdom is a guide for me in almost everything I do. His humor and wit have made the difficult things in life more palatable. He is gone now but my last words to him when he could no longer speak were, "Gerald, as long as I am alive you will be, because I will pass your wisdom on to all who will listen."

My two closest friends, Denise Goldman and Valerie Wojciechowicz who have held my hand and walked with me through very painful and difficult times as well as through breakthroughs and triumphs. For them my gratitude runs very deep.

Then there are those without whom, there would be no "Dragons to Butterflies." The instigator was Suzi Henry. Without Suzi sharing my first book, *Taming the Dragon,* with Ruth Frushour, then bringing me a book to read by Chip St. Clair, author of *The Butterfly Garden,* I may have not have been inspired to write again. It was Suzi's willingness to listen to hour upon hour of my stories while I was sorting out what needed to be used and what didn't, along with her endless hours of reading and rereading my writing, that kept me going. All who gain anything from reading these pages can be grateful to Suzi.

To Martin Dahlborg, who gave up many lunches and other extra hours to help with technical issues and brain-storming.

There are so many more: Debbie Naeve, Julie Miller, Don Smith, Mary Padlak, George Lewis, Eric Gentry, Barbara Miller and David Sutton (another book). My life has been and is rich with teachers and friends.

Then, first, and last is the Unconditionally Loving God of my understanding, who held my hand as I went through hell and half of Georgia.

Finally, to all those who read my writings, for you I am also grateful.

INTRODUCTION

By Ed Cooper

When I was asked to write a brief introduction by the author it seemed that I was stalling or at least procrastinating. My dilemma however, was attempting to condense a 31-year friendship into a few paragraphs. Johnnie and I share many common bonds, experiences and likes. One of these is an appreciation of old movies, and westerns in particular. We have often compared our relationship with that of the two main characters in the *Lonesome Dove* series by Larry McMurtry.

Augustus McCray and Woodrow Call, two men with lots of personal baggage trying to live principled lives, do the right thing and speak the truth even when the choices to do so are personally painful and difficult. At the age of 62 I can only recall 2 or maybe 3 relationships in my life that have been as close, honest, intimate and personal as that which I share with Johnnie.

We met when I was 30, 1 year new in twelve step recovery and both without much of a clue.

We grew up together, made many mistakes, struggled, learned, and became men. I've watched Johnnie follow many different paths. I have watched wrong turns, meltdowns, hospitalizations, failures, and lots of successes. I have never seen him quit.

I am also privileged to be one of very few who have known most of Johnnie's family, including his father, sisters and several nieces and nephews. My impression is that they are all remarkably strong, resilient people. Each has their own story of coping and survival and I have a deep respect for them all.

My name appears somewhat frequently in this book. Prior to the writing, my friend had the courtesy to ask how I felt about some of the events depicted in this book, in particular, my lapse back into drug abuse after many years clean. During that time our roles reversed and I became the one in need of help and guidance. In retrospect, I believe it was harder on Johnnie and my loved ones than me.

From the time we met many years ago, Johnnie's focus has been on the spiritual principle of honesty. It has been a constant in all our time together. That being said, I'm absolutely comfortable that whatever is written about me is the truth whether I remember it exactly the same or not.

Having history with people is a priceless commodity to me. Other than my wife of 39 years and my children, there is no one I have a closer bond with. The writing of this book has been a catharsis for both of us. I read each chapter usually the day after it was written. Though I knew most of the stories, I never had heard them told consecutively over the course of a life. Tears do not come easy for me, nor is it a comfortable place. I'm way too tough for that. I've had to choke back emotions too many times during this writing process and frankly its beginning to piss me off!

This book has the potential to help many people who are suffering in silence and think they are alone, particularly children. Few people are willing to talk about their experience of child abuse, even less about sexual abuse. It's especially difficult for men. It is a demonstration of courage to bring these dark shameful secrets to light. I too was a child victim at age 4 and never told a soul till I was 30. It's been painful but healing to revisit my past via this book. I hope this book will have the profound effect on others that it has had on me.

In the beginning of this intro I mentioned *Lonesome Dove*. At the conclusion of the series Gus is dying of sepsis and his friend Woodrow visits him. To sum up their lifelong friendship, Gus says, "It's been one hell of a party, ain't it Woodrow?" Though our party is not yet over, I feel the same way.

Johnnie Calloway is my friend, my brother, and a fellow traveler on this journey of life. My life is better and richer for his being in it. I am deeply grateful that Johnnie was there to help pull me out of the fire.

With deep affection and appreciation

Ed Cooper
Johnnie's Twelve Step Sponsor

CHAPTER 1

THE GUILT

Standing on a chair and drying the dishes as my momma washed them is my first memory of her. I remember folding towels with her after she had done the laundry. I loved helping her. I also remember the day they were burying President Kennedy. I was really upset that I couldn't watch *Captain Kangaroo*. The procession was on every channel. Yep, all three channels. She stood in the hallway with a broom in her hand and explained to me the importance of what was happening. I think she cried.

I remember walking to and from work with her, holding her hand and feeling safe. It seems like she always rubbed my back until I went to sleep at night. I always felt secure when she was around. I was totally a momma's boy. I went everywhere with her and making her happy was all I cared about. I would fight to the death for these memories because they are the only ones I *want* to remember.

But then came the day she had to go to the hospital for a checkup. I begged her to let me go. She just said, "No, Momma will be right back." I didn't understand. I went everywhere with her, so I pleaded, "Please let me go."

"No," she said, "It's just a checkup. I will be right back." But she *never* came home!

I've been told that she was in the hospital about six months. When they finally realized that she was dying, she decided she needed to see her boy, so my grandmother and sisters sneaked me up the fire escape. (At that time you had to be fourteen years old to visit in a hospital). It was about six floors up. That fire escape was scary, but not scary enough to keep me from going to see my mom.

I remember how heavy the air felt and how cold it was when I entered that hospital. It also stank, and the color of the walls was this ugly, dull, and depressing off-white, almost yellow color. Thinking back, it was probably because they were stained with tobacco smoke. There was a horrible energy and everything was so drab and dreary that I immediately wanted to leave. This was before we were even in her room.

The day she left for the hospital she had looked as healthy as anyone, but when I walked into that hospital room, full of anticipation to see her, what I saw was horrific. This woman did not look like my mom at all. I did not know what death was at the time, but even to this five-year-old it was obvious that she was not long for this world. She was very pale with a chalky-white complexion and was very thin. But worst of all was that huge blister on her lip. I can still see it like it was yesterday; a big yellow scab on her upper lip. It actually looked like snot. It was disgusting. I turned my back on her and walked to the end of the bed. I was so incredibly disappointed. I had come to see Momma, but she wasn't there.

I wanted more than anything to just leave. I remember her saying something like "Please get him out of here. This is too hard on him", and "He shouldn't have to see me like this." Then she said, "Come give Momma a good-bye kiss."

I just said, "No, I don't want to."

I had no idea what those five words were going to do to my life. I was so confused. How could anyone say that this person was *my* mother? My mom was very pretty, and she laughed and smiled a lot. This woman couldn't have laughed or smiled even if she had something to laugh or smile about. Somewhere inside me, though, I knew she *was* my mom and that something was very wrong.

When we got home, my sister, Jackie, told my drunken dad what had happened. He became very angry and pulled off his belt and spanked me, all the while screaming at me, "Here your mother lays on her deathbed and you, her only son, won't even kiss her good-bye". Not even Alzheimer's could erase that memory from my mind.

The next time I saw her, she was in a box in a funeral home, lifeless, with a powdery mask of makeup that someone had put on her. It was horrible and smelled putrid. To the best of my memory, Momma never wore makeup.

Everyone, even my dad, was dressed up. All the men had on suits and ties, the women wore their church clothes, and they had dressed me and my sister in our Easter outfits. I hated those clothes and to this day I won't wear a tie. We were there for the *viewing*. What a stupid thing to do! I still think that the whole *viewing* concept is insane and morbid.

There was a long line of people that kept walking by her, most of them crying, saying all these really nice things. What was really crazy is that they kept saying, "Doesn't she look nice?" My thought was, *'Hell no. She doesn't even look like my mom!'* Someone mentioned how honest she was and how much she loved her children. Even at the age of five, I thought, *'I hope when I die people can say, "At least he was honest".'* I became acutely aware of the importance of what is said about

3

you at your funeral and somewhat obsessed with what legacy I would leave.

Next was the slow ride in that long line of cars to the cemetery. There were so many people there. Again, I had no idea what was happening. But what came next would stay with me forever. Everyone was gathered at this big hole in the ground. Almost everyone was really crying now. My sisters were sobbing terribly, and I didn't understand why. Soon they were lowering the same box that I knew had *MY MOM* in it and the preacher was saying all this gibberish. Then he asked someone to throw the first shovel of dirt on it and people kept doing so until I couldn't see it anymore. And then she was gone. It took a long time for me to understand the finality of it all.

The driveway to my grandmother's house was gravel, so you could hear immediately when someone pulled onto that drive. I was eleven years old before I stopped going to the front door to see if it was Momma coming home.

As time passed, I began to see the result that her not being around was having on my entire family. And it was all my fault. I was the one who didn't kiss her, and that was why she left and why I got spanked. It was my fault that my dad beat my sister and would do things that made her make those horrible sounds from her bedroom when he went in there and closed the door. Most of the time when he went in there, I would hide in the closet and wrap my arms around myself and rock while I cried, saying over and over again to myself, 'You chickenshit. You should protect her. You should stop him! You're just a coward. A real man would stop him.' I would do this until the screaming stopped.

There were also times when I was missing my mom that I would go into my grandmother's bedroom and close the door. I had to hide since I was a boy. Boys weren't supposed to cry.

For some reason, I needed to *see* myself cry, so I would look in the mirror while I did it. To this day I do not understand the importance of that. All I know is that seeing my own tears comforted me.

While crying, I was constantly apologizing to her, saying, "Momma, I am so sorry I didn't kiss you. If you will just come home, I will kiss you forever." And inside I was screaming, '*Momma, please come home!*' The pain wasn't just emotional; it was physical as well. Because I couldn't let anyone know I was crying, I held back making any sound and would just do it silently. This caused my throat to hurt all the time and my stomach stayed in a knot. I would stay in my grandmother's room until all the tears were gone and then pull myself together and try to act as if nothing happened.

Momma had kept a log of my life in my baby book. Everything I ever did was recorded in there: my first steps, my first word (Momma), who was at my first birthday... everything. Often I would get that book down and read it. It was like Momma was reading it to me, and I felt loved. My baby book allowed me to feel connected to her.

My mother's dog, Bridgette, nearly grieved herself to death. She would not eat. She just laid on the porch and looked sad. I would talk to her and try to get her to play with me, but for the longest time, she just laid there. I would walk off and she still just laid there. I would talk to her and say things like, "Momma didn't leave us, girl. God just took her home. She still loves us. We will be okay." At least this is what the good church folk were telling me. Then one day I got up to walk away and Bridgette got up and came with me. From that day until she died, she followed me everywhere. We were the epitome of the dog and boy story. She walked me to the school bus every morning and would be waiting for me when the bus brought me back.

She was always having puppies. I mean *all* the time. It made my dad very angry that she had so many. Most of the time we would just give them away but she had so many that we ran out of friends to give them to. Then my dad would take them down some old country road and drop them off.

Even that wasn't enough. One day I got off the bus and Bridgette wasn't there. I immediately freaked out. I ran all over the neighborhood calling her name. I shouted until my voice was gone. No one had seen her, or knew where she might be. My best friend was gone! She was the only one that understood the pain. I could let that dog know the truth. I could go off into the woods or into some isolated place and cry with her. She understood and she was now gone too.

I found out later he had taken her and dropped her off too. According to my grandmother they had taken her down to the 'bottoms' where we had to go to get legal liquor because we lived in a dry county. The bottoms were twenty six miles away! She was gone, never to be seen again. GOD had taken her too, like the good church folk had said. I was constantly asking myself, 'What did I do that was so bad? Now I don't get to have a mother or a dog.'

One week later ... she came home! Bridgette had found her way twenty six miles and come home! I was so excited! 'Maybe God did like me.' Even my dad said, "I don't care how many 'fuckin' puppies that dog has, she'll never leave here again." The very next day, she was run over in front of the house. She had come twenty six miles, down roads she had no way of knowing, only to be run over in front of the house. I was so angry. People say kids can be mean, well so can adults. One of our neighbors just had to tell me that when she was run over puppies were scattered all over the road. They buried her while I was at school. Everybody told me that no one knew who ran her over. It wasn't long before I found out ... it was my neighbor. Before that I had really liked him. He was a really good dad to his children, and tried to be as nice to me as he could. After he ran over Bridgette and lied to me about it, I literally hated him. Trust, for me, was getting more and more difficult all the time. No one ever told the truth, no one ever did what they said they would do, and no one could truly be counted on.

I took responsibility for everything. It was my fault that my dad had to drink so much. After all, I had taken his wife from him, which meant it was my fault that he was so angry that when he was drunk he would beat up the people I loved. I remember at least three times that he broke my grandmother's arm. He would beat my sister with his big thick leather belt until there were welts on her back. Then sometimes after he beat her, he would take her into the back room and close the door. To me, none of this would be happening if I had only kissed my mom. Everyone said that God had taken my mother to be one of his angels but I knew the truth ... 'He didn't take her, I did!' What God did do though, was take Bridgette as more punishment for me holding back that one kiss.

Once during the rainy season in Western Kentucky, there was a tornado that devastated one of our neighboring counties. I was riding around with my grandparents and the man on the radio said that a little girl had been killed during the tornado. I was in the back seat when I heard this and I started crying, trying not to make any sound and whispering, "What did I do now?" My grandmother heard me and asked, "What's the matter Son?" I responded, "I don't know what I did now but I didn't want that little girl to get hurt." She told me, "Johnnie, you didn't have anything to do with that girl dying." Somehow in my guilt-ridden mind that tornado and that little girl's death were my fault. Everything was that way.

I started acting out very early. I was caught stealing the first time when I was six. Coming home from school on the last day of the school year, the bus stopped for refreshments at this little country store. All the kids but me and my sisters had money for treats. I stole some baseball cards and other candy and got caught and in trouble. I do not remember the consequences, but whatever they were, they didn't even slow me down. Soon after that I started breaking into people's houses and stealing stuff; just anything, it didn't really matter what it was, although baseball cards were usually my focus. I was about nine or ten when the stealing got really bad.

All this and I was still getting good grades in school. I made straight A's and A+'s until halfway through the fifth grade. The day I got my report card for the first semester of the fifth grade one of my dad's drinking buddies and childhood friends came by to visit. When he saw my report card, he went on and on about how good I had done and then gave me a quarter for each A. I thought almost immediately, 'If he knew I killed my mom, he wouldn't give me these quarters.' My next report card was all D's and D-'s. No one noticed, not even my teachers.

I started acting out in class, being the class clown and wrote a lot of sentences for talking during class. I almost never got to go to recess, got at least one paddling a week and became very popular with all the wrong people. According to my teachers and other peers, I was just being another Calloway. I heard the phrase often, "One of those damn Calloway's that will never amount to anything." I set out to prove them right. I had already acquired a 'What the fuck.' mind-set. I cursed a *lot,* and I could not complete a sentence without the f-bomb. Cursing made me one of 'the guys'.

After my mother died, my sister, Jackie, who was five years older, took over the mothering role for me. She was very protective. When my dad's fits of rage would come and he would be beating grandma, Jackie (my ten-year-old sister) would grab me by the arm and lead me to grandma's closet where we would sit on granddad's trunk and cry. One day Jackie stood up and said, "I have got to get out of here. I am not going to live in this closet anymore." I pleaded, "Sissy, please don't go." She just had to go; she couldn't bear the thought of hiding anymore. From that day forward she would always try to protect my grandma, even though grandma would often turn on her and throw her under the bus.

I was the only kid in school that the bullies avoided because they were afraid of my sister. She always had my back. There was one day in particular, in the fourth grade, when I was in a big argument with an 11th-grader over her. He was telling me how good the sex was with her and I was trying to fight him. He just placed his hand on my forehead and held me back and laughed. Then, out of the blue, there was this big thud. She had come into the gym and saw what was happening and clocked him in the head with a softball. His ear bled. That was just one of many times she stepped in to protect me.

She was kissing a boy in the back seat of the bus once and I didn't like it, so I hit him on the back of the head with my huge social studies book. I didn't know they had their tongues in each other's mouths. They almost bit each other's tongues off. That is what it seemed like at the time. The guy came after me and Jackie stopped him.

Another time I had stepped on my Aunt's toe, accidentally. I didn't have a shirt on and she slapped me on the back. According to Jackie, she left welts on my back bad enough that you could see the finger marks. Jackie flew into her like her life was at stake. Even my dad said later that he thought Jackie was going to pull out every hair in our aunt's head.

Unfortunately, when she became my *mother* she also became my dad's wife; cooking, cleaning and constantly being taken into the back room. He always closed the door. All I could hear was her crying. The whole house would become dark and cold while they were back there.

As a result of what was going on for her at home, Jackie became very promiscuous at a very early age. She dressed really provocatively. At that time miniskirts and make-up were very popular. My sister wore her skirts very short and her make-up very thick. She never needed the make-up. Just to add insult to injury, she was very beautiful and therefore all the guys wanted her. Just to add to my guilt and confusion, so did I. I loved her now more than anything, and the fact that she was so attractive didn't help matters. What was happening to her with all the guys and with my dad left me really mixed up about right and wrong, when it came to sex. For me to *want* my sister, I knew was wrong; although no one ever told me it was. And being jealous of her boyfriends made me feel sick inside.

Most of the memories of my childhood are very vivid. But my memories of the sexual things that my dad did to me are more like hazy shadows or silhouettes. My mind has not allowed me to clearly remember much detail when it comes to that. In fact, I am so committed to putting only the truth in this book, that I am a little hesitant to talk about what I don't *clearly* remember. But to leave it out entirely doesn't seem honest either. So, what I do have are a few *very* vague memories of physical sensations, like gagging, and an incredible uneasiness and dread about having to share the same bed with him. Also, I felt really ashamed because I can kind of remember that there was a degree of pleasure in what my dad was doing to me some nights.

The fact that my own dad was doing sexual things with both me and my sister was way more than my young mind could make sense of. So in the same way I blamed myself for my mom's death, I turned all this confusion into even more self-hatred.

I was consumed with guilt. 'If I hadn't killed my mom none of this would be happening to my sister.' Even my mom's dad was constantly telling me that momma wouldn't have died if she hadn't given birth to me. "The pregnancy was just too much for her." Two of my aunts also echoed this remark. I heard one say to the other, "Janie knew she would die if she had another child. The doctor told her she wouldn't survive it." ... or something to that effect. My thoughts after hearing that were, 'Momma loved me so much even before I was here that she was willing to die for me and I wouldn't even kiss her goodbye.' I ran immediately to the old milk barn down the street and berated myself and cried for I have no idea how long.

We lived in a small two bedroom mobile home where privacy was non-existent. My sister had a bed in the back of the trailer and my dad and I shared the smaller bedroom in the middle of the trailer. It was a single bed so it was very small. I will never forget the closet built into the wall (my second home) over three drawers. He always made me sleep against the wall so I couldn't sneak out of bed and go sleep on the couch. I had to learn to sleep without moving, I never knew what kind of mood he would be in when he woke up. If he had come to bed drunk anything could happen.

I always considered myself an Indian. My senses were so magnified. I could lie in my bed and tell what mood he was in by the sound of his footsteps. It was vital to know his mood so I could know whether it was time to hide in the closet or not.

If I could get to the closet and get in it before he got to the room, there was a chance of safety. The phrase 'Out of sight out of mind.' was very real. I always slept with the proverbial one eye open. The truth is I do not think I ever really got to sleep. The fear was overpowering and it made breathing almost impossible.

CHAPTER 2

THE FEAR

In our home there was the constant sound of screaming, shouting and cussing. Everyone cussed and the f-bomb was in every sentence. These things and the sounds of flesh on flesh were frightening but the most terrifying (as rare as it was) was the silence. Silence was the warning that the crap was about to hit the fan.

Around the age of nine, I woke up at my grandmother's house and the light was on in the kitchen. Someone was in there. Actually the energy in the house let me know there were two people in there. There was a low whisper, but even that was scary. They had never been concerned before about waking anyone. Frightened and alert, I wondered why they were being so quiet. No one was getting into the fridge or rifling around in a cabinet for something to eat ... nothing.

My dad was a loud drunk. When he was drinking and eating it sounded like pigs eating slop, making all kinds of slurping noises. I hated to hear him eat. It was disgusting. If someone was around it was embarrassing.

There was no way he could be in that kitchen and make no sound. I could always feel his presence and I could always tell if he was drinking. The air just felt different. The house felt eerie. 'What was going on?' I was terrified!

Curiosity got the best of me. I got out of bed and slipped down the hall, being as quiet as I possibly could. There was a knee wall that separated the kitchen from the hall, so I got on my knees and crawled to the end and peeked around the corner. When I saw them, I gasped and was immediately frightened, thinking they had heard me. No, they hadn't, and I sighed in relief. There he sat cool as a cucumber with his right arm raised. Under his arm he was bleeding like crazy. My grandmother was standing there wiping the blood and trying to sew him up. She would pour a little whiskey on it, give him a drink, wipe it and stitch. To watch her with that needle and thread was scary. She had obviously done this before.

They were speaking in a whisper that neither of them ever used. Even my grandmother was a very loud person. Being loud was important in our house. It was a show of power and if you didn't have it, you just got run over.

Listening closely, I learned what had happened. He had been in a knife fight with someone and was afraid to go to the hospital in fear of being sent to jail. Evidently the other guy had been wounded as well. It was terrifying to watch as she wiped and stitched and he just grimaced and took it. He seemed scarier than ever. To know he could just 'grin and bear it' made him seem unreal. She finished sewing him and for the next while he wore shirts with sleeves but he came out okay.

Throughout my entire childhood the fighting was constant. He beat on everybody, except me. I have no actual memories of him hitting his step-dad, Poppa. Poppa made sure he was always out of sight, usually in the yard, sitting under a tree, squatting like a frog. His nickname was Froggy because of that. Usually he was drinking, and to avoid being in the house, he kept his beer stashed outside, and would just drink it hot.

Poppa was a very small man, and quiet. He loved to fish and I loved to go with him. We all loved Poppa and I always felt bad for him.

We *all* lived in terror. You never knew what was going to set my dad off. We walked around on pins and needles all of the time and it took its toll. It was really difficult for me since I was an attention seeker who was terrified of being noticed.

Jackie got the worst of it. If any of the rest of us did something to get his attention, she would create a distraction and take the beating. This made me feel guilty and worthless. I was the man who was supposed to be protecting her, not the other way around. My fear would paralyze me and I would hide in my closet and cry quietly until my throat would hurt so bad I couldn't do it anymore. My eyes were sore all the time from the crying. All the while I was telling myself repeatedly that I was a coward, that a real (seven-year-old) man would protect his family.

One day he was about to get on Jackie. In the process of his shouting, he said something about her crying. She became very stoic and said with a glare in her eye, "Motherfucker, you have had the pleasure of making me cry your last time." He pulled his big thick black belt off and he had that look in his eye. When he was angry his eyes would go black and if you looked into them it looked like no one was home. They were deep and empty. He started to spank her. I cried immediately, but not Jackie, not one tear. She never moved. She just stood there and took it. I do not know how long he spanked her but I knew if she would just let him win and start crying he would stop. I begged her, while sobbing, "Jackie please just cry." She would not! He finally stopped. She had won? It didn't look like winning. Her legs were almost bleeding and the welts were everywhere.

From that day on whenever he wanted to spank her she would fight him. She fought him like a man and for her anything was a weapon. If she could get her hands on it and get it to move, it was a weapon. She hit him with books, with lamps and pans but she would no longer just take the beating. He eventually came to respect her. When they would go at it she would get the same look in her eyes that he did and it would be like two wild animals. Sometimes her anger frightened me as much as his did.

They never actually cut one another but they were always pulling the big knife out of the kitchen drawer and threatening each other. Then came the day they were fighting in the house, screaming and calling each other names. He was slapping her around and she was hitting him with whatever. The noise had become so constant that it was like background noise that got dismissed. The rest of us were in the yard and the whole neighborhood could hear them. Frequently our neighbors would call the police, but not this day.

I knew something was different about this fight and was afraid for my sister but I dared not interfere. I hated myself for being afraid enough of him to let him beat on her and my grandmother. We were all out in the yard acting as if nothing was going on and then we heard the gun shot. It scared the hell out of us. Jackie came out of the house screaming, "That crazy son of a bitch just shot at me." I was so relieved to see her upright and so afraid of him coming outside. He never did and it ended just as it had started, from nothing.

Jackie had been out with her friends one night She was already partying, drinking and drugging and as usual, dressed very provocatively. There was a lot of family at our house that night; aunts, uncles and cousins. When Jackie came in they all started in on her, calling her a slut and a whore. Usually that would prompt a big fight. Tonight she was silent. I will never forget the silence. She never said one word, but went right to the bathroom and when she came out she had cut both wrists ... bad. The blood was gushing from both of them. I was in total shock. I have no way of remembering the exact amount but to my young eye it seemed the blood was shooting three feet in the air from both wrists. My dad said, "Who the hell do you think is going to pay for this?" Then everyone else started in on her. No one seemed to even notice that she was bleeding. This was the whole family, not just my dad. Even my grandmother never suggested calling emergency. Jackie was starting to lose her color when I finally said "Would someone help my sister?" It was all I knew to say. With that alarm my grandmother woke up, got something (I don't remember what) and tied her arms off and took her to the emergency room.

The fear was constant and there was never a moment of respite. It wasn't just my dad. My grandmother was a real issue as well. After my mom's death, my dad got a settlement and a monthly social security check. He used the settlement money to buy our single-wide trailer. He moved it into my grandmother's back yard. I am grateful for her taking us in but she could not be counted on.

Sometimes when he was beating her she would get away long enough to call the police. They would come arrest him and damn if she wouldn't jump in her car and beat them back to town to get him out. I once asked, "Why the hell not just let him stay in there for a while?" She responded, "I just needed a break." Even as a kid, before I knew anything about my dad's life, I knew, she had hurt him some way and her guilt was why she allowed him to do the things he did. I later found out why.

If we did something while he was not around, she would store that info until she needed it. She would hold something over our heads, sometimes for months, and then out of the blue she would tell him and his wrath would be diverted from her to one of us.

Jackie finally reported him for what he was doing to her sexually. My grandmother took her to the judge's house for the report. He allowed her to stay with our (maternal) grandfather. That was like getting the fox to watch the hen house. When her court date came and it was our grandmother's turn on the witness stand, she said Jackie had made it all up. The judge made her come back home.

The fight that day was horrendous. My dad was enraged but Jackie had become a force to be reckoned with. I was horrified of what was coming but in the end it was no more than the usual, busted lips, black eyes and other bruises. She was only thirteen!

Soon after her day in court, she ran away. The day she left I begged her to let me go with her. She said, "no", and promised me she would be right back. I didn't see her again for a very long time, just like with my mom, another promise broken and I learned *women don't come back*.

They found my thirteen year old sister in Nevada, all that way from Kentucky, working in a topless bar. She was sent to reform school. The place she went was shut down years later for child abuse. Jackie still doesn't like to talk about the things that happened there.

After Jackie left, it was just the two of us. You would think he would have taken the back room with the big bed and given me the middle room with the small bed. No, he still made me sleep with him.

It was horrible. In bed with him I could never really sleep. If he came to bed drunk I was too afraid. If he wasn't drunk, I didn't want to disturb him. Most of the time I just lay there and wished I could sleep. Sometimes after he passed out I would cry myself to sleep. Trying to cry quietly was almost impossible.

Going to school with no rest wasn't easy. Acting as though nothing was happening was even more difficult. I knew other kids who had troubled homes and the State had taken them and put them in foster care. Even though things were as bad as they were, I did not want to lose my family. I had also heard about what happens in foster homes so I chose to stay with the fear I knew.

One night (when I was eleven) he came to bed drunk and made me lay next to him. He rolled over and started kissing me, sticking his tongue in my mouth. I couldn't stand it anymore. I got up and ran up to my grandmother's house and woke her up and told her what had happened. She put me in the car and took me to the judge's house just like she had done with Jackie. The judge turned me over to my grandfather … out of the frying pan into the fire.

My day in court came and I believe to this day one of the hardest things I have ever had to do was to sit on that witness stand and tell about what my dad had done to me, WITH HIM SITTING THERE JUST STARING AT ME with that hollow look in his eyes!

Then it was my grandmother's turn to testify. She said I was lying. No one questioned it, no one said, "Isn't it odd that this is exactly what happened with his sister?" They all just wanted to act as if it never happened. They reversed the decision for me to live with my other grandparents and sent me back to that trailer.

I felt so betrayed by my grandmother. I was confused. I could not understand why she said what she did or why she turned on me like that. She took me home. He stayed in town and went to the bootlegger. I went home and the fear was so intense I could not be still. I had no one to turn to. Jackie was gone and at this point I certainly wasn't going to turn to my grandmother, and Clifford (my mother's father) was not an option.

The fear that I felt constantly kept my stomach in a knot and affected me physically. My bowel movements were never regular. I didn't know then that it meant something was wrong. I thought it was normal.

When he finally got home, he was so drunk and angry that he was slobbering and almost foaming at the mouth, calling me names and acting like he was going to hit me. Drawing his hand back and screaming like he had always done with Jackie, only he never actually hit me. In all those years of living in that fear, I had never been as afraid as I was at that moment. I knew he was going to kill me. I was sitting in the big chair in my grandmother's house trying to cover my head and my face so that if he did hit me I wouldn't be bleeding like Jackie always had. He grabbed my arm, jerked me out of the chair and dragged me crying back to the trailer. I wanted my mom or my sister or someone to protect me. There was no one … just me and I was too afraid to protect myself. Once we got to the trailer, he threw me into the chair, stood over me and kept screaming, raising his fist and acting like he was going to hit me. I swear every time he raised his hand my heart stopped and I thought my life was over. He never did hit me but the rushes of fear each time he raised his hand were overwhelming.

He finally said he was hungry and he was going to get Momma to make him something to eat and when he got back he was going to take care of me.

Good! I was going to get a chance to run away. When he left I ran to the window to watch him go around the corner and as soon as I could no longer see him, I was out the door. I don't think I had ever run as fast as I did at that moment. The problem was I had no idea where to run. I just ran. None of my family was to be trusted. Any one of them could turn on me and just bring me back to him. Once I got to the end of the street, I really did not know where to go. I was in one of my friend's back yard trying to decide. I literally ran in circles thinking, 'Down the road to my aunt's house or into the field to get in our secret tree house?' Not being able to make that decision I continued to run in circles. My friend's mom just stood in her window and watched.

Next, I saw him walking down the road to find me and I ran even faster in circles. My grandmother was now in her car and looking for me. I think this time she knew I was really about to get it. She passed him on the road and when she got to me I was torn about whether to run to her car or not. After all, it had been just a few hours before that she had turned on me. I didn't know if she was coming to help me or just looking for me for him. I eventually ran to her car because I didn't know what else to do. This time she was coming to help. After this round with him, the threats of hurting me became more frequent and very believable.

The 'elephant in our living room' was actually in the front yard. Everyone in our neighborhood knew what was going on in our house with the beatings and all, and they were all just as afraid of him as we were. I don't think they were aware of the sexual things he was doing with Jackie and me but they had often called the police on him for the violence, and just made sure the call was anonymous.

I eventually became the family crackerjack box. I was passed around every few months from one family member to the next. With me came my mother's social security check. One hundred eighty three dollars a month was a lot of money to feed a child. Everybody wanted access to that check. I created a real resentment for money and the seeming power it had over people and what seemed like the fact that *it* was always wanted more than I was.

Every time I moved I had to immediately adapt to a whole new set of rules. What was okay at one house was totally unacceptable at the next. The fear of not getting it right or getting the rules confused was constant. The feeling of rejection was always present. I never felt I was enough.

With every move came a new school and the first few days of school were always about the guys trying to find out where I fit in the pecking order. A fight everyday was unavoidable.

I was not a good fighter. I could not bring myself to hit anyone in the face. I hadn't been able to since I was ten and one day my friend, Stevie, and I were play-wrestling, like Hulk Hogan and Dusty Rhodes. My dad was walking home drunk and saw us. My friend had me pinned down and my dad came over and looked down at me and asked, "What are you doing?" Stevie outweighed me by thirty or more pounds. I answered, "Me and Stevie are wrestling." He said, "But why are you down there?" I responded, "Stevie is winning." In a very gruff voice he now said, "You had better get up." Stevie and I both knew what that meant. If I didn't get up I was going to be in big trouble. We wrestled around a bit and Stevie let me get on top. We had put on a pretty good show. Now I had Stevie pinned. When I started to get up, my dad said to me, "Where are you going?" I answered him, "Home." But he wasn't satisfied, "No, you are not done here." He made me hit Stevie over and over. I busted his lip, his nose and eye. I think I made an internal decision in that moment that I would never hit anyone again and I would never be like him.

When I started having to fight in each new school, at first I could not really defend myself because of this pledge I had made. So I learned real quick how to be a pretty good wrestler.

The fear in my life was horrendous and was always accompanied by guilt. It was all turned inward and I punished and hated myself more than anyone else could ever have. This created an anger within that eventually consumed me.

CHAPTER 3

THE ANGER

I was so angry with God. I hated Him more than anyone or anything. I was told He ruled everything. He took my mom! He controlled everything and in my mind He was not helping me and my sister at all. They said I needed to love Him and turn to Him for help. Yeah right!

I was angry with my mother for leaving me, with anyone who I thought could have rescued us and didn't, with Jackie for leaving me behind and with my Aunt Diane and Uncle Jerry for abandoning me. Everyone I tried to love … always left.

There was a period of time when my aunt and uncle would take me to their house every other weekend. It was like teleporting from hell right into heaven. Their world was so different than mine. We laughed and played and she would hold me and tell me how much she loved me. It was almost like having my mom again. They wanted their own children really bad but she kept having miscarriages. When I was about nine, she finally had a pregnancy that took. They had a son. After he was born there were no goodbyes, no discussion … nothing. They just never invited me to their house again. I didn't see them again for many years. Still with all the anger over the loss and betrayals, the one I hated the most was me.

I was angry with everyone that said they loved me, or anyone who said they were my friend. I did not trust anyone! The more someone said they cared, the closer they were watched. My revenge was theft. Once someone told me they were my friend or that they cared for me, soon thereafter they lost something that meant something to them. Usually it was something they really cared about. My dad had always said, "Do unto others before they do unto you, and they will always do unto you." What he didn't say was, "And I'm the one who will do unto you the most."

Even though I was convinced that my mother's death was my fault, a part of me knew that was crazy. But why the hell else could all this be going on? What the hell did we do to deserve this, if it wasn't because I killed my mom? Damn! The conflict between logic (somehow knowing, even as a five-year-old, I could not possibly be responsible for my mom's death) and insanity (believing that by not kissing her I killed her) was infuriating.

Anger was necessary in my family. It was like air and water and you couldn't survive without it. My anger scared me so I pushed it inward. I could take the pain and I should, because they didn't deserve any more hurt than they already had. I was more afraid of my own anger than I was anyone else's. I was afraid it would engulf me and make me like him/them and Momma would be even more disappointed than ever.

My anger came out sideways and more often than not I would hurt myself in some way; hitting my head against the wall, never enough to do visible damage, just enough to ache. I would frequently punch myself in the stomach until it hurt. The self-inflicted pain felt like a payment for my wrongs, a penance for the disappointment that I was to my mom. Even though at her funeral I wanted more than anything to be remembered for being honest, I couldn't tell the truth if my life depended on it. I hated myself for lying, knowing that wasn't what she wanted for me or what I wanted for myself.

So my attitude settled in on 'fuck it. If you can't beat 'em join 'em.' I was so angry knowing what I knew she wanted me to be and even if I was, no one cared. She had always been so proud of me and that made me want to do the right thing. Now it just didn't matter. I hated myself more and more all the time and reached a point where I was too ashamed to even think of her.

I stopped asking her to forgive me. So much of what I was doing was unforgivable. I was getting into trouble in school, talking all the time, clowning around, doing whatever I could to make the other kids laugh, and then having to stay in detention instead of going to recess. I had discovered that making people laugh was my reason for being and if I could, then all was good. I was constantly getting paddled for my foul language. I was always in scuffles with the other kids in school, which was really difficult being I was afraid all the time.

I hated myself for not being able to fight like my dad and Jackie. I was an embarrassment to my family because Jackie had always come to my rescue. It had also been embarrassing to me that no one would mess with me because they were afraid of my sister and I was pissed off for being afraid and needing her to rescue me. I always felt so little.

I was angry about all the mixed messages around me and all the missing parts. I felt like everyone else's mothers had told them some great secret about life and school, that my mom didn't get a chance to tell me. She *had* told me, at least, that I was a "good boy", but still I was being punished so terribly. I often thought, 'I must have been an outlaw on another planet and sent to earth for my punishment.' Maybe that's why I started misbehaving so badly; so my crimes would at least match the consequences.

I hated having to lie about my dad's work. I wanted so badly to be able to tell my friends that he was something other than a maintenance man at a cemetery (sometimes). He would work just long enough to get booze money and then he would quit. The people who ran the place loved him because he did such a great job and made the grounds look beautiful. That's why they allowed him to quit and come back, over and over. My dad was just too drunk most of the time to work a steady job. Instead, he would usually just play poker and find or steal stuff to pawn for more whiskey.

I hated that he could go out on Saturday night dancing and I would wake up Sunday morning with a new mom. Hell, he would do this without divorcing the previous one, then tell me I needed to call this new drunken witch "Mom." These women were alcoholic sots. I was *never* going to call them "Mom"; my one act of defiance. Even he couldn't get me to betray her.

I was like a pressure cooker about to go off all the time. The anger turned to hatred, the hatred was self-directed because it was all my fault and my whole family was living in this nightmare because of me. I started wanting to die around the age of nine, not suicidal (that didn't come until later), I just wanted it to be over. The pain in my stomach from holding all this in was excruciating. It was a very physical reality. It hurt and whenever it wasn't there I would hit myself over and over. I thought I was supposed to hurt and no one knew.

Momma would have known. She paid attention to whatever was going on, but now there was no one paying attention. If she were around Jackie wouldn't have to be playing wife to him or mom to me. If she were still around my dad wouldn't be so angry, my grandmother wouldn't be getting beaten and I could again be a good boy. I would wonder, 'How many times am I going to have to scream (silently) that I am sorry?'

One night around eleven o'clock after he had been drunk for several days, my dad was having the D.T.'s (delirium tremors). These were very common at our house. They are the result of drinking too much for too long and the body reacts to the alcohol, or the lack thereof. My dad only had friends who drank like he did and the ones that had to deal with the D.T.'s would come to our house for my dad and my grandmother to nurse them through. Several of my dad's friends ended up dying while having them; luckily, never at our house. This night, while my dad was having them, there wasn't anyone else there to help him but me. He didn't have anything else to drink and usually one of the things they did was to give them little sips of whiskey until they were settled down.

He asked me to go to the bootlegger for him and get Reagan to front him three half-pints. It was late and dark and we lived about four miles out of town, so I hitchhiked to town to get the goods. I was scared to death. I was only eleven and it was the first time I had hitchhiked without him. We had hitchhiked several times together but this time, I was by myself and it was dark. On the way there I had a moment of absolute brilliance. 'He won't know how many I get. He is totally out of it. I am going to get six (three for me and the guys, three for him) and we can get good and drunk tomorrow.'

The next day was the first time I got drunk. It went just like this: I drank, got drunk, blacked out, passed out, came to and wanted to do it again. From that time forward I drank as much as I could, as often as I could, for as long as I could. Prior to that first inebriation my head was like a radio stuck between two stations. Once I was drunk it dialed into one station. Even though it was a very self-destructive station, it was at least only one station. After that the road got very dark. Somehow though, for the first time I felt like I had some control and a voice. Instead of just listening to all their abuse, I fought back, at least verbally. All to no avail; it was all moot but at least I was standing up.

I was furious with my fifth grade history teacher. She told me that before embalming fluid was used, people sometimes were buried alive and they knew this because as farmers were plowing their fields they would uncover a wooden casket and the person inside would have their hands up by their heads and their hair in their hands where they had come back to life and screamed themselves to death. That may not be the exact story she told but it was definitely the picture she portrayed. After her story, I had nightmares for a very long time. The nightmare played out just as she described it and I would wake up in a cold sweat with the vision of my mom pulling her hair out and screaming, "Help me." ... and I couldn't. Now on top of everything else, my mom had been buried alive and gone insane in that damn box.

I always heard from my family, "The Calloway's just never get a break, we're cursed." And the community saying, "He's just one of those damn Calloway's and he will never amount to anything." 'What the hell did we do to deserve this curse?' Once, while at church, I heard the preacher say, "Only a few are chosen." I could not imagine what I needed to do to get on that list. 'Why me?' Or 'Why not me?' were constant questions in my head. Oh yeah, I killed my mom, and as insane as that seemed to me even as that confused child, that was the only thing that seemed to make any sense. There had to be a reason and it couldn't be just bad luck.

I absolutely hated my mother's father, Clifford. I had more anger with him than I did my dad. He was crazy! In nineteen seventy-two Motown was really big. I loved the music ... it made me *feel*. The Chi Lites had a song, "Have you seen her?"

The song started with a poem. Those words pulled at my heart. I just had to start writing poetry *but* ... I was a male Calloway in Kentucky. I would never live it down and I would embarrass my whole family if anyone knew I had these feelings. The guys in school would laugh me out of town. So I wrote and I hid the poems. Anytime I was alone in my room I was writing poems. It was the only place I could get all those feelings out.

My granddad found them! I do not think I will ever forget sitting at his kitchen table when he came in and threw them on the table and snickered, "You must be one of those damn faggots. Men don't have these feelings." Then he tore them up and said, "No one can know about these." I continued to write them. I just hid them better.

Living with Clifford and my grandmother, Momma Trixie, was a nightmare; not physically, but mentally and emotionally. His mind games and the way he manipulated people with money was confusing and frustrating as hell. And I could never figure Momma Trixie out either. On one hand she was the epitome of a grandmother, coming to my rescue when Clifford was on one of his rants, a great cook, and slipping me money to go to the movies (I used the money to buy alcohol). My quandary was trying to imagine why such a nice person was married to such a jerk.

He was always trying to get us to choose him over our dad. For instance, my dad wouldn't get me a bicycle so Clifford did. I only had it a week and it was stolen. A couple of weeks later we were at Clifford's house and he and Dad were drinking. I was pilfering about his garage and there was my bicycle. I ran into the house, "Wow! You found my bicycle!" He said, "No, I didn't find it. I knew where it was all along. I paid Charlie fifty dollars to steal it." The damn thing only cost thirty five dollars, new. I asked, "Why would you do that?" He said, "I drove by one afternoon and your sister was on it. If you promise she will never be on it you can have it back." He tried to pit me and my sister against each other. So I told him, "If my sister can't ride my bike, I don't want it." I never got it back. But … my dad was actually so proud of me that he sold something of my grandmother's to get me a bike.

Also, when living with Clifford, his means of punishment was to take us to see the judge. One day I had been playing basketball five miles away on my bike and was five minutes late getting home. Once in the house, he said, "Go get changed. We are going to town." Translated, that meant we were going to see the judge. I didn't argue. It was pointless with him.

When we sat down before the judge, I was still thinking, 'I was only five minutes late!" The judge, Herbert, asked, "What's he done now Clifford?" Clifford said, "I do not know what in the hell I am going to do with him. He is drinking three gallons of milk a week." Herbert snickered, looked down at his desk, trying to get his composure. Once he did, he looked up at me, obviously still trying not to laugh and said, "Johnnie, son, you are going to have to slow down on the milk."

I was astonished and embarrassed and thought, 'Seriously? You brought me to see the judge over milk? And, you, son of a bitch … the State gives you one hundred and eighty three dollars a month to buy my milk!' In nineteen seventy-two, one hundred eighty three dollars would buy a lot of milk.

When Jackie lived with him, he tried to rape her at least once. That did not work in his favor. We had no safe place … everywhere we went was the same.

Later I had to explore that whole idea about being a faggot to see if he was right or not. That was not a long lived experiment. I discovered very quickly that I loved the female form too much for that. Being with a guy was too much of a reminder of the things that had gone on with my dad.

The anger that I carried about sex ruined my puberty. I was terrified that I would do 'it' wrong. One afternoon while living with Clifford, my dad and my stepmother came by. They were well on their way to being drunk. They had been swimming and she had on a bikini. I was fourteen. She was not a very attractive woman at all but she was almost naked and I *was* in the middle of my puberty.

They asked if I could go home with them and my granddad said "Sure." That was not the norm, because he and my dad hated each other with a passion, and neither of them ever said, "sure" about anything. There was an energy about the whole thing that was compelling. I wanted to go.

Not long after we got to their house my dad passed out and Linda asked me to go outside with her to see the chickens. There were *no* chickens. I thought that was weird and let it go. We went back inside and she soon asked, "Want to go see the garden?" There was *no* garden.

What she did next was disgusting and horrifying at the same time. She dropped her bikini bottoms and asked me to kiss her there. My dad was just inside the house! If he caught this he would KILL me. I said, "No."

I started back to the house and she took me by the hand and led me to the bedroom. Next thing I knew we were doing it. I was terrified he was going to wake up and I just wanted to get off her but I was fourteen and it felt good. The fear of him waking up was too much. She got frustrated with me being in a hurry and pushed me off her and said, "I am going to go get your dad to finish what you started." I hadn't started anything.

My young heart was consumed with guilt, fear, anger and confusion and the path I took as a result was long and very dark.

CHAPTER 4

THE RESULT

Throughout most of my adolescence I was suicidal. If I didn't have someone to entertain or make laugh, the darkness would settle in and I just couldn't bear the pain. I lived in my own little world. I lied about everything. It was better than the truth. I was drunk or high as often as I could afford to be and it was never drunk or high enough. I drank to the point of black-outs all the time. It was the only way I could handle the self-hatred. No one's parents wanted their kids around me. It was no longer Jackie's and Daddy's reputations that were killing me, it was my own. I was doing a great job of proving all the people right that had said, "He's just one of those damn Calloway's…"

I stole from everyone. Nothing was sacred and the people who were trying to help me were the ones that I went after the hardest. I hated them because I knew they were just setting me up in order to let me down. "Do unto others before they do unto you." This was now my motto as well as my dad's.

I was getting arrested all the time for petty little crimes and misdemeanors (never anything serious just *a lot* of small time stuff). I was sneaking out of whichever house I was staying in at the time to go get drunk or high or both. The loneliness

I felt was heart wrenching. Being out at two o'clock in the morning and thinking, 'It's two o'clock in the morning and no one knows where you are and no one cares.' I was only fifteen! With all the other emotions, the guilt, the anger, and the fear, the loneliness was the most painful. I had turned against the world. No one in it could be trusted and no one followed through with their promises. Everyone that said they were there for me either left or made sure that I did.

I was constantly disappointed in myself. My mom had taught me to be helpful and to care for others. I was being anything *but* helpful. My dream was to be a hero and to rescue someone from harm's way. I was very destructive in everyone's life and I hated myself for what I was doing. I always wanted to help and I couldn't.

Most of the time I was either at my dad's place or my granddad's. To this day I cannot tell you which was worse. Whenever I was staying with Clifford he was constantly taking me to see the judge. He never tried to discipline me himself. The first time I went before him I was thirteen. He said, "I am not going to put up with the same things from you, that I put up with from your dad and sister." He locked me up in the drunk tank, an eight foot by eight foot cell with no light and I believe there was a hole in the middle of the floor for going to the bathroom. It was meant to be a scare tactic. It did not work. I wore it like a badge of honor. It was my rite of passage. I had grown up with men who were in and out of some type of jail/prison or sent somewhere for their alcoholism, all the time. I had already accepted this to be my lot in life. Now that I had been arrested and put in jail, I was just one of the guys and I had arrived.

School was my only safe place, even though I was in trouble all the time. Being able to make people laugh and not being afraid made it worth it. I was in fights all the time (even though I wasn't very good at it) but I couldn't allow myself to walk away. The fear of someone knowing I was afraid was worse than the fear of getting beat up. I had rather get beat up than embarrass my family name by walking away. Walking away would have made me someone's punk.

Since I was constantly changing homes and schools, the first few days of each new school there was fighting the tough guys; a difficult thing to do without being able to hit anyone. I would always try to wrestle them to the ground and get them to leave me alone. It would work most of the time but there was usually a black eye or busted nose in the process. I hated fighting but I had to do it anyway. My family had a reputation that had to be protected. How many times had I heard my dad say, "We are Calloway's and we ain't afraid of shit!" Then he would look at me and say in that gruff voice, "Right?" Trembling I would respond, "Hell no!" I don't think he ever noticed the shaking or maybe it was just on the inside, but I was terrified that he would see my fear. So I became a very good actor, capable of bluffing anyone with my false bravado. In school it was often said. "I can't believe you stood up to them." No one knew my fear.

Although in school, I only had to be afraid of a little skirmish, no one really got hurt. A minor black eye or busted lip but never anything like the blood that flew around the house. No one's arm was broken and no one was carted off to jail. It just wasn't the same. Even though I was scared that I would be found out, school was still a much safer place to be. There was very rarely any laughter in our house. At school there was a lot of laughter, and I loved that I was usually the one who could get it going.

In the tenth grade there was yet one more school and a fight everyday for the first three days. After the third day and third fight, I was at the water fountain spitting out blood. One of my teachers, Mr. Richards, came over and leaned on the wall by the fountain and said, "You know? It's not really any of my business but it seems to me that you need to find another way to impress these kids. This doesn't seem to be working out very well for you." I actually laughed. Mr. Richards then became my friend. I loved that man.

Mr. Richards knew me like a book. He was my English teacher and my study hall teacher. In his classes for some reason I felt especially safe. I had not really ever done well with English. He realized that I did like math though and he made sentence structure a math equation for me. I still didn't like it very much but I wanted him to be proud of me so I tried harder and did much better.

Things at home still sucked. In the tenth grade I was living with my sister Marsha and her husband. He was great!!! He really tried to teach me things. He would take me to work with him and try to teach me about drywall and painting. He even tried to teach me how to shoot a bow and arrow. I wanted to do better with everything and make him proud. I was tired of the craziness and here I could have a fresh start.

One night I went with a friend to the bowling alley. I was supposed to be home by a certain time and I was late. Marsha asked, "What the hell happened?" I told her, "We had a flat." She freaked out and started screaming at me, "You are not going to get by with the same shit here that you have everywhere else." I was telling the truth, we really had gotten a flat. She grounded me for six months. I threw my hands up and said, "Fuck it! No matter how hard I try I will never get it right."

A couple of weeks into the grounded time I made my first real attempt at suicide (age fifteen). The family had gone to some friends' house and I was home alone. That was never a good thing for me. I was my own worst enemy and no one could treat me or speak to me any worse than I could.

That night I truly gave up. Marsha and I had been arguing. She said, "You selfish little shit. All you care about is yourself." I will never forget how that felt. I wanted more than anything to be able to let the people I loved know that I loved them. It just never seemed to show up in my actions. I was never going to be the person my mom would want me to be, I was never going to be one of the good guys. I gave up that night and cut my wrist.

History has a way of repeating itself. Marsha came in soon after I had cut my wrist and once she saw what I had done she said, "You selfish little son of a bitch. Who do you think is going to pay for this?" Just like with Jackie, and just like with me, my niece said, "Momma can we help Uncle Johnnie?" She was five at the time.

One day (before I was sent back to Clifford's) in Mr. Richard's class, he was giving a lecture on Helen Keller. I usually listened to Mr. Richards but this day I was too obsessed with who in class would show up to my funeral if I did commit suicide because they cared and who would come just to get out of school? Mr. Richards abruptly stopped his lecture and asked, "Johnnie what do you think about Helen?" I was always honest with him and being honest really felt good. I responded, "I'm sorry Mr. Richards, I wasn't really listening." "I know," he said, "Some people listen to my lectures and some people just sit in my class and wonder who all is going to show up to their funeral." I freaked out! He knew what I was thinking! I said, "Don't worry Mr. Richards, from now on I will pay attention."

He knew what I was going through and he cared. I was really hurt over losing him the next time I had to move.

Next, it was back to Clifford's house and summer. I was introduced to Pam cooking spray as a way of copping a cheap buzz. The stuff was incredible, a total loss of consciousness ... my cup of tea. When I was high on Pam, the only thinking that was going through my mind was the buzz. I wrecked my car one day while huffing Pam. There was a policeman, that I already knew on a first name basis, Bob", behind me. I had been driving all over the road and finally ran off the road and pinned the car against an embankment.

The weird thing about the Pam buzz was you caught the buzz immediately and you could come down immediately. As soon as I saw Bob's badge in my window the buzz was gone. He told me about my crazy driving and that I had almost ran a little girl over by her mailbox. He asked me what I was on. I replied, "Nothing, I think I had a seizure." He searched my car and only found the Pam can, thought nothing of it and let me go without my car or my license. He also instructed me to go to the hospital for some tests before I could get my license back.

I was horrified that if they ran any tests they would discover Pam in my system and the whole town would know. I ran away to find Jackie. I thought she was in West Virginia. I had seventeen dollars and I had never been out of Mayfield, Kentucky. I hitchhiked the entire night to go somewhere I had never been, looking for my sister who I hadn't spoken to in over a year.

I arrived to Huntington, West Virginia in the middle of the night and found a boarding house for six dollars a night. In Mayfield, if you are looking for someone, they are usually easy to find because it is so small that everyone knows everyone else's business. 'This should be easy. Just ask around a bit and someone will be able to direct me to my sister.' Everyone I asked about her looked at me like I had three heads. I was starting to think about some kind of robbery since I needed to eat. I went back to the boarding house. Checkout time was eleven. There was a community shower and I needed a shower bad. When I came out of the shower there was a little old lady sweeping the floor. Taking a glance at me she said, "Son you sure look lost." I quickly responded, "I am. I came here from western Kentucky looking for my sister and no one seems to know her. I am broke now and have no idea what to do." She asked, "What is her name and what does she look like?" I answered, "Jackie Corns." Before I could describe her the lady interrupted with, "Little bitty thing about this tall?" while holding her hand at about Jackie's height. "Sometimes black hair sometimes red?" Immediately I felt relief, someone at least knew her. "Yes! That's her." Then she said, "You are luckier than you think. She works at the topless bar just around the corner. Let me finish my job here and I will take you over there." My heart sank and raced all at the same time. It broke my heart to think she was working in one of those places again and yet I was also excited to go to one of those places.

The old lady finished and we headed out to the bar. The owner/bartender told us that yes, she had worked there but she had quit. Then stated, "She is in Dallas." 'Oh my God' I thought, "What the hell am I going to do now?" Then he said, "She calls me every other day because I owe her money. She didn't call yesterday so she will be calling today." I quickly responded, "Okay I will just wait." The place was full of half naked girls. He laughed, "Oh no you won't. Here's some money. You go eat and watch a movie then come back later. I will get a number from her so you can call her."

She did call and she had the guy get me a plane ticket and we met up in Dallas. The next morning we quickly turned around and headed back to West Virginia. I believe the reason we left so quickly was that she robbed the guy she was with. As soon as we got back, I became the live-in babysitter. Jackie had two daughters. One was around three years old and the other around one and a half. I was just over sixteen and had no real business with these two. They were safe enough, but I had no business taking care of children when I needed supervision myself. I was home with the kids all the time.

One night she decided to give me a night off. I didn't know anyone, so I went looking for her to hang out. I found her, I am not really sure how, but I did. She was in this little diner and she bought me a burger. This guy behind us spoke up and said to *my sister,* "I've got the money honey if you've got the time." Jackie kind of glanced over her shoulder and went, "shhh." At first it struck me as odd but I didn't think anything about it until he said it again. I was enraged! I turned and said to him, "You can't talk to my sister like that." Jackie interrupted and shouted to me, "If you want to keep eating and getting those model cars and comic books, you will shut the fuck up." Then she started in on him. They had a few words that led nowhere.

She had a room over the diner where she did her business. We ended up in that room and I was telling her it had to stop. We had never screamed at each other, to my memory, but we were now. I was physically much bigger than she was. I picked her up and threw her across the bed and she never hit the floor. She shot back across that bed like she had been shot out of a cannon. In about two seconds she had me pinned on the floor. She had this move like it was from some kung fu movie. She had thrown her leg behind my knee and slapped me in the chest. I went down like a dropped rock. She reached into her bra, pulled out a straight razor, and laid it on my throat. Her eyes were hollow and she looked like *him*. She said to me in a very calm voice, "I will not take from you what I took from him. If you ever put your hands on me again I will cut your throat like a stranger on the street." My sister was no longer in that room with me. That thing that she could become when she reached a certain level of anger was what I had to contend with. I threw my hands up in surrender and said, "OK."

I left West Virginia right then and never went back to her place to get the things I had acquired or to say goodbye to the kids. I just started hitchhiking back to Kentucky. I was not going to be able to live there knowing what she was doing and how she was supporting me. She had been my substitute mom for so long and now, I had just found out *this* mom was a prostitute.

This meant another trip to Clifford's and another new school. This time though, I would make my mark some way other than fighting. Drugs! Clifford had boxes upon boxes of pills stashed away in a cabinet in the back of the house; Elavil, Talwin, Yellow and blue Valium. Now I was the man!

In the orientation I embarrassed the principal, which scored me a lot of points. In the middle of his speech I got up and started walking out (my first day). He said, "Young man, when I am speaking I expect my students to sit down and pay attention." My response was, "I know and I am sure that what you have to say is very important but right now I have got to piss." The whole school (all twelve grades) busted out in laughter and I was 'in' with no fights. I had no idea what that day was going to bring about. The principal now had it in for me.

I had been to the new school only three days and was voted "class favorite". They *really did* vote me "class favorite" and I didn't think they even knew my name.

With the drugs, the laughter and now a car, I was in. I still hated myself no matter how cool I made everyone else think I was. Now more than ever, I was an embarrassment to my mother and I had two nieces, who I absolutely adored with all my heart and I was a horrible example for them. I was supposed to be their hero! Rena, (Marsha's daughter) and Lee Ann (Jane Ann's daughter) became my reason for being. There is no way for me to know how many times I didn't act on my suicidal thoughts because I didn't want to leave them that legacy. I never wanted them to know the extent of my drug and alcohol use. With everyone else, I pretended not to care. I did care and deeply, I just felt terribly powerless over the curse of being a Calloway and the guilt of killing my mom.

The suicidal thoughts were becoming more and more prominent and there was not enough drinking or drugging to stop my self-loathing. It was taking more and more drugs to cause a blackout. I was doing every kind of drug that was put in front of me. There was no drug of choice. I did anything that was available, even the ones I didn't necessarily like. I was selling a lot of drugs at school but no pot. I didn't have a connection for pot. I just sold the drugs I stole from Clifford.

One day the two guys that I ran with the most, were caught smoking pot at school. We were always high at school. The principal told them if they said I sold them the pot, he would see to it they would not get into any trouble. Even though I hadn't sold it to them, I felt I needed to be punished for all the other drugs I had sold anyway and I just accepted this betrayal as part of *the life*. I let this one slip by. I had forgotten the rule,

"Do unto them before they do unto you." I never was mad at them for that. I had come to expect it from people.

I was barely sixteen and I spent thirteen days in a six by six cell with a cot, a sink, and a bible. They took me out once to be analyzed by a psychiatrist. While I was in that cell, I had a lot of time to think and for the first time I knew I needed help. I knew that I was my own worst enemy and that I was going to die before I turned twenty-one if I didn't get that help. Somehow I knew my friends had done me a favor because if something hadn't happened I was going to kill myself.

After thirteen days I went once again to see the judge. As I sat before him, his first words were "What do you have to say for yourself?" My response was, "I am my own worst enemy, I need help. I am not going to make it. I need discipline." He looked puzzled. "If you think you need discipline, I have just the place for you."

The Boys' Camp reform school was the next stop. The first day there was insanely frightening. I had long hair, super bell bottom jeans and a strut. I *needed* these guys to see I wasn't afraid. This time, with them, the act just was not good enough.

As I sat in this big chair with my coolest look, the guy across from me shouted, "SIT UP IN THAT CHAIR." I sat up as if God himself had given that command and I tried to smile. "TAKE THAT SMILE OFF YOUR FACE. YOU GOT NOTHING TO SMILE ABOUT." I took it off. The other guys started to filter through the main room. As they passed me, "What's your name?" "Where you from?" "What you in for?" Everyone was screaming.

It seemed they all had acne really bad. I had never had a pimple. I was terrified that this was going to happen to me. They all looked so angry. Of course I had all the fears that most would have had and I was petrified that I was going to be gang raped.

I was escorted to this big room by one of the camp members, with his hand in my belt. I found out later that this was called 'being on stick'. It was to keep anyone from going A.W.O.L. In the room there were several staff members, five group counselors, each group leader, the receptionist and myself.

Later, I came up with my own description of the 5 groups which went like this: A-group, "the Big Babies"; all really big boys who tried to be scary but were really Teddy bears, B-group, "the Pretty Boys"; who thought the answer to everything was to comb their hair, C-group, "the Runaways"; who thought the answer was to get the hell out, D-group, "the Bullies"; who, no matter what happened, would hit something or someone and E-group, "the Runts"; all the little guys.

In the room I was interviewed extensively by everyone in it. They were all very stern. The interview was to determine which group I was going to be in. C-group was the decision. I was given 'my states', the uniform we wore during our stay. By now the entire camp was in the common area. All sixty guys were screaming at me. My knees were visibly shaking. In all my time with my dad and all that craziness, this was *real fear*. There were just too many of them. They were like piranha and I was the meat just thrown off the boat.

I was escorted into the shower room and the whole damned camp came in to watch me change and to yell at me. "WHAT'S YOUR NAME?" "WHERE YOU FROM?" "WHAT ARE YOU IN FOR?" They were all around me, standing on their toes and screaming. My knees gave out and I fell there in front of all of them, in only my underwear. They didn't stop. They were relentless. Then there was a little break in their screaming and they started to step aside to make way for this really big black guy. My terror was through the roof as he approached me and he leaned over me sitting on the floor and said in this surprisingly gentle and soft voice, "Don't let these punks scare you, man. If you stood up and screamed back at them most of them would crap their pants."

Later I discovered his name was Tommy. He was quiet and kept to himself most of the time but everyone seemed really afraid of him. I did not understand why. He seemed like a kitten. We were only supposed to know what the guys in our own group were in for. There were certain guys though, whose stories got out anyway. Tommy had been an honor student and an athlete growing up in the hood. He was really trying to *not* live that life. He had a very abusive step father who was constantly beating on his mom. Tommy came home one day from school to yet another beating but it was to be the last. Tommy beat his step dad to death with his fist. Once I learned this, Tommy was immediately my hero. Although it also added to my guilt about not helping Jackie. "Why the hell didn't I do something like that?"

The Boy's Camp ended up being one of the best things that ever happened for me. There was no predetermined amount of time for your release. There were four steps that you had to complete. The time it took to complete these steps was on you. You controlled your own fate.

The staff there really seemed to care about us and they were totally consistent. When any one of them said, "If you do this ... this is what will happen ..." It happened! There was no discussing it and no excuses. The promised consequence had to take place. I thrived! I loved knowing what the rules were.

I truly excelled, became a group leader by vote and moved right on to the camp counsel. I had a voice. My opinion mattered. I was respected, not only by my group and the camp, but also by the staff. I got to speak my mind about the scare tactic used upon arrival that lasted for the first few days. I told them how unnecessary I thought it was and how much time it wasted. I told the staff that most of us were already scared to death. They actually heard me! Once I voiced this to the staff (almost immediately), the scare tactic was eliminated. I had never been as proud of anything in my life. I was learning about respect. These men were showing me how to be a man.

The place was rough and the lessons came hard but I somehow knew this was necessary in my life. They would give us projects for our consequences. One of my projects was 'the tree project'. I do not remember what my misdeed was but I will always remember the 'tree project'. I was taken to a tree on the property that they said was *my* tree. My task was to cut it down, cut it into firewood, carry the firewood up the hill to the camp and stack it. Then … dig the stump up and dig another hole to bury the stump in. Now my tree project was completed. I took great pride in that project.

Another time the shower room floor was my project. Our project usually only lasted until we told them what they thought you needed to say. What they were asking me about this time was a lie that had been told on me. I could not provide a believable answer for the lie. I was on my knees for eighteen hours scrubbing that floor. After I finally collapsed they had my group members, one on each side of me, hold me up, while another two got on each side and worked my arms for me. I finally came up with a story they believed and it was over.

They trained us in how to be part of a team and how to work together. I always believed and still do that they were retired drill sergeants. Everyone in a group was responsible for the whole group. If one of us got out of line the whole group would get consequences; such as not getting our mail, losing recreation time, movie night and phone calls or worse yet, no visitors. We had to look out for each other.

There were four steps required in order to complete the program. They were: your life's story, future plans, group's opinion, and camp's opinion. When I left I was the second fastest person to ever get out of there; one day short of four months. The day I left, I sobbed! I could have lived there the rest of my life. I was safe there.

The only one of the four steps that was an issue for me at all was step two; future plans. I wanted to go into the military. They would not take me because of my drug charges. My group leader, Mr. Johnson, tried every way he could to help me get in because of my ability to conform and follow rules. They just weren't having it with my drug experience. At that time I had never wanted anything more than to be in the service.

Finally, it seemed like the authorities were on my side. They were not going to allow me to go back to my dad's house or to Clifford's house. The only other option was foster care. After hearing the horror stories my group members had shared with me about their foster homes, I really did not want that option.

So along came Jane Ann, who is my mother's daughter from her first marriage. I had only seen her a few times and never realized she was really my sister. She was so different from the rest of us. She didn't cuss, didn't smoke or drink. She finished high school and went to church. I always thought of her as an aunt or something. I know I had been told who she was, but it hadn't sunk in. She was the one 'white sheep' in our family.

Jane Ann and her husband showed up as my visitors one weekend at the camp. I really didn't understand why at first. They sat with me and my group leader, Mr. Johnson, as we discussed my options; which were very bleak, to say the least.

Jane Ann then asked if I would consider living with them. I was stupefied. 'She doesn't really even know me. Why would she even think of that? Doesn't she know my history?' There were so many thoughts that ran through my head so fast, and so many doubts. 'What the hell was she after?' Then I remembered the check. 'Everybody wants that damn check!'

Jane Ann came prepared. She did know my history, including how everyone had always been after the check. She then pointed out that my check was my money. They wanted no part of it. It would go into a checking account with only my name on it. I could not imagine what her angle was.

Jane Ann was my only viable option. I couldn't just get a job at the Boys Camp and stay there on site. I had to leave, and soon. Off to Jane Ann's it would be; a new home ... a new set of rules and a clean slate... kinda.

CHAPTER 5

THE BREAK

Now I was at Jane Ann's house ... a new home and a new life. I had no idea what to expect. It was like being dropped onto another planet, with no idea about how to act. Jane Ann was incredible. I fell in love with her and the entire family immediately. I didn't necessarily fall into trust with them though.

I think Jane Ann had to go to classes at the Boy's Camp and be taught what to expect from me and how to handle whatever may come up. At the camp I had been taught how to identify my feelings and the importance of talking about them. It had become something that I actually liked to do. It felt so good in the camp to be able to let out what had been confined inside me for so long.

Jane Ann would sit up and talk with me until the wee hours of the morning, processing all my fears about being back around my friends and in society. We talked about my fears of not being accepted in our church and being judged, and how I was afraid that I would make it difficult for her family by being around. I loved them and they all loved me and I still felt like I just didn't belong there. Regardless of how much they did to make me feel like I was a part, those old haunting voices,

"Just a damn Calloway that will never amount to shit.," were still with me.

At the Boys Camp I had received my GED, with flying colors. I now had a diploma and had only finished the tenth grade. One of my release restrictions was that I could not go back to any public high school. That was very depressing for me because I loved school. I wanted a chance to make it right. A goal I had committed to in my future plans step, and which the Camp had approved, was that I would go to college. I took my SAT test and passed it. Done! I was off to Murray State University, right out of the tenth grade and reform school.

Not having had eleventh or twelfth grade English, there were some things I missed out on; very important things, like learning to write term papers, essays, etc. My English class in college was the only class I had where there were kids with whom I had gone to high school. On our first day the teacher announced, "I want you all to write an essay." I totally freaked out. I had no idea what it was that he wanted me to do. Here I was again. The teacher was walking up and down the aisles looking over everyone's shoulder to see what was being written. Once he got to me, he stopped. I was doing nothing. He asked, "Having a difficult time with a topic?" I motioned for him to lean over so I could whisper to him. He did and I said, "I have never written a paper." He rose up and said aloud, "It usually takes awhile but I have found him on my first day; the class clown. Well sir, if you have never written a paper, you'll just have to take special education reading and writing." He may as well have said, "You'll be riding the short bus."

The kids that were in there from my previous schools, who knew me to be the class clown, immediately broke out in laughter. College lasted eight weeks for me and I quit.

I was under a ton of pressure. Being at Jane Ann's was great but I never felt I deserved it and I never really trusted it. I couldn't believe that someone/anyone loved me without wanting something back. But they *never* wanted anything except to love me.

Even though Jane Ann talked with me about everything, there were certain things I didn't feel safe to talk to her about; my fear of trusting the love; my fear of relaxing; how deep my fear was that it would all just go away or that I would do something wrong and be made to leave. I was even afraid to trust all the laughter and we laughed a lot.

We were constantly playing pranks on each other. Once when I went in to take my shower, Jane Ann sneaked into the bathroom and stole my underwear and took them and sewed one of the legs shut. I got out and tried to put them on and the whole family was standing outside laughing as I was hobbling around trying to put them on. When I realized what was happening I laughed harder than any of them.

The whole situation was very foreign to me. I thought of myself as some wild animal that these people had decided to domesticate. Prior to Jane Ann's home I had spent my entire life sleeping with one eye open. Now? Nothing to be afraid of? Fear had become a habit. I was afraid not to be afraid. My fear seemed to have protected me all those years. It kept me alert. I really did not know how to be without it.

We went to church all of the time. I was treated *great* there. I was like a poster boy for the bad boy gone good concept. One girl's mother asked me to take her daughter out! I didn't go out with her but I did start dating the Preacher's daughter!

Lori, I think I really loved her but I had no reference point to know for sure. We went everywhere together. She was beautiful and a lot of fun. I was still afraid of the whole sex thing. Linda (my stepmother) had really done a number on me.

Lori and I got engaged. I was terrified. At some point she was going to find out. Even though I had never had a date, I don't think anyone would have thought I was actually a virgin. In high school I had a lot of girls who were friends but never any more than that. Seventeen years old and I had been in jail many times, had been best friends with many of the popular girls in school and I was still a virgin. And now I was engaged. She was definitely going to find out the truth.

The break from my old life didn't last long. I don't think I was at Jane Ann's house but about four months before I folded under the pressure. Trying to have a job, trying to teach Sunday school, trying to do the right thing, I felt so out of place. It may not have been so but I felt like a lot of the kids were looking to me to be some kind of example. I wanted to be a good example more than anything. All my life I had fantasized about being the good guy, wearing the white hat. So here I was ... I had the white hat on, I just couldn't get it to fit.

The guys that I had partied with all those years, laughed whenever I would say no to going somewhere with them. Constantly, almost chanting, "Let's see how long this game lasts?"

Lori wanted something from me that I just couldn't give. She found someone who could and I fell off the wagon. I was off to the races. The break was over. And the beast was unleashed.

CHAPTER 6

THE BEAST

In the Boy's Camp, they said I might be a drug addict. At the age of thirteen my counselor had said I was probably an alcoholic. But no one ever told me what that really meant, much less what could, if anything, be done about it.

I have heard a description of the alcoholic/addict that goes something like this: 'Inside the addict/alcoholic person there lives a beast. The beast has a ferocious appetite and simply must eat.' The addict/alcoholic lives with the fear, 'feed the beast or be eaten by the beast.' The depths that an addict is willing to go are totally contingent on their beast's appetite. Some may abandon all sense of right or wrong and do not believe that this goes without consequence. I have battled the beast my entire life and for me the beast has had many heads because my addictions have been many; drugs, alcohol, gambling, sex, food and relationships. There are probably others but the point has been made. I have heard many say that they were addicted to anything that made them feel good. Personally I have been addicted to anything that helped me to feel *nothing*. Feelings were a luxury I could not afford.

In my mother's notes in my baby book (which by some miracle I still have), she had written that I had thirty convulsions in my first week. Today they would be called seizures. They put me on Phenobarbital and I was on that drug for over a year. Phenobarbital is a barbiturate and is very addictive. Add to that a predisposition to addictive tendencies, a family history of alcoholism, and there isn't much room for doubt; I was an addict/alcoholic before my first pill or my first drink.

Some say addiction is a disease. The truth is it does not matter to me if it is a disease, if I got it from a toilet seat or from drinking after another addict/alcoholic. The bottom line is I am an addict/alcoholic and have been for as long as I can remember.

No one who ever tried to help me, (Jane Ann included) ever stood a chance. They were up against all the scars of my childhood and the beast … an almost unbeatable pair.

Once the drinking and drugging started at Jane Ann's, it was like I was trying to make up for lost time. I drank and drugged with a vengeance even though in my heart I really did not want to. Nothing was off limits. With the drugs and alcohol came stealing, lying and everything else.

My heart was breaking for what Jane Ann's family was going through but I had no *off* button and I didn't seem to be able to do anything else. The absolute agony of not wanting to use and not being able to stop, only another addict/alcoholic could ever truly understand. Loving them was not enough, appreciating them was not enough and no one could have ever wanted to do the right thing more than I did. I wrote this poem in nineteen eighty-two, while shooting bathtub crank. Maybe it will get the point across?

I care
And don't know how to show it
I love
And can't make people know it

I want to do good and don't know how
But if things were different
If it could show
If I could do better
And if they could know
See I've been my own prisoner
Who longs to be free
Can't seem to escape
And let me be me

After the beast started to scream for me at Jane Ann's, I fed it and the self-loathing was all over me again. This time it was worse though. There was no one to blame. They were all good to me. They did everything to try and get me back on track. I couldn't do it. It was torment, wanting something so badly, something that seemed to be in my control, but I couldn't stop. It was utter hell.

I got a job at K–mart, overseeing the patio department. I had a lot of "Blue Light Specials". Basically, I gave things to my dope friends for dope. Needless to say I got caught, got arrested and went back to jail. If it had been fifty cents more it would have been a felony. God was always watching out for me.

One of my visiting days, Jane Ann and my youngest niece, Capricia, came to see me. We only had a small steel window to look through for our visitors, and I was devastated when I saw that child looking back at me through the hole. Capricia said, "Uncle Johnnie you didn't have to steal that money. I would have given you some of mine." I told Jane Ann to get her out of there and not to ever come back. At that moment I wanted to deny that any of my nieces or nephews existed. While living with Jane Ann and her kids, Lee Ann, Brad, and Capricia, I felt like I was their hero. And yet, I was a horrible example.

They were always so happy to see me, "Uncle Johnnie, Yay!". They were constantly crawling on me, wanting to play and be near me. But after the drinking and drugging started back up, I just wanted to hide from them. In fact I wanted to hide from everyone. I was so embarrassed and humiliated about my powerlessness over the drugs. At that point my suicidal thoughts became all-encompassing. I didn't think a human being could feel as low as I felt at that moment. I later learned, I could go much lower.

I was in and out of jail all the time and working for a farmer named Gerald, who taught me how to work in tobacco. He was constantly getting me out of jail. I thought of him as a dad. Hell, I just wanted anyone to be that for me. Gerald was the closest thing there was.

I loved working in the tobacco fields. I was good at it and took a lot of pride in it. It also helped that being hung over while working was accepted.

I was back and forth to Jane Ann's and lived off and on with some of the other farmers I occasionally worked for. The time line of the events in my life from the ages of twenty and twenty-three are a little hazy. There was a phrase from the sixties, 'Reality is for those who can't handle drugs' that fit me to a tee.

I was stoned all the time. When I drank I wanted to blackout. If I could remember what had happened the next morning, it had been an unsuccessful night. I woke up frequently in places I could not identify, with people I did not know and several of those times were in some jail, not even knowing what county I was in. In Mayfield Kentucky, I went to jail so many times for public intoxication that my nickname became "Rudy's boy". Rudy was the jailer.

The tales of my battles with the beast are tragic but some of them are absolutely comedic. I ran with some of the dumbest criminals known to man. Tragedy and comedy added together can make for one hell of a tale. The timeline is out of order here, I think. These stories happened between nineteen seventy eight and nineteen eighty, from about age eighteen to twenty, but not necessarily in this order.

I reached a point where the word "job" seemed to be a four letter word and work was out of the question; almost like it was beneath me. But the beast still had to be fed. I did almost anything to feed the beast. I stole pop bottles from the back of this one store, carried them to the front and sold them back to the same store. I was really depressed when they stopped taking deposits for pop bottles. Those bottles kept me drunk for a full summer.

I actually took fifteen dollars to one of the local banks and opened a checking account. Things were different then. I went to the shoe store next door to the bank and wrote a check for the fifteen dollars and cleared out the account but now I had a checkbook.

After that I would go into a store and buy a thirty dollar item, (a coffee pot or something), leave with it, come back in an hour and return it. They always gave me cash back, never the check, and I was off to the bar. I ran out of the checks in that little starter book they gave me from the bank and started using counter checks. In those days the stores kept blank checks from the local banks, in case you ran out of checks or left your checkbook home. When I got to the counter with my item, I would act surprised about not having my checkbook with me. They would ask what bank I used and give me a blank check for the determined bank of the day, I would write the check and make up an account number and off I'd go. I wrote twenty eight of those checks.

One day one of my drinking buddies asked me, "Man how do you stay in enough money to stay drunk? You don't have a job." I told him about my check game. He wanted to try it. I said "Go ahead." He asked if I would go with him and let him know where he needed help. He was in one checkout line running the scam and I was in the next listening very closely so I could coach him afterward. When my friend was asked, "What bank?" His response almost put me in shock, "It don't matter."

It did put the cashier in shock. She told him, "I need to go clear this with the manager." He was extremely excited! To him this meant it was working. When she left to go speak with the manager, I stepped over to his lane and said, "Man you better get the hell out of here." He was still excited and was actually convinced it was working. He told me, "Stop being paranoid."

I promptly left my transaction and the building, went outside to sit down and watch the show. A few minutes later two policemen walked into the store and walked back out with my friend in tow.

Then Mayfield got their first Narcotics Detective. I had been arrested for a breaking and entering charge and he and another detective said they would drop the charges if I would help them with a particular drug dealer. They said they would give me one hundred dollars a week to buy drugs with if I bought them from this dealer. Every Friday for over two months the Narcotics Detective would meet me down the street from my grandmother's house and give me the money, and I would make up stories for him about the drug dealer. I wasn't about to tell him the truth. It was fun (a lot of fun). He even gave me a business card to use as a "get out of jail free card". Also, I had the guy in question fronting me the drugs and I was using the money from the Detective to buy my booze and other drugs.

I ventured off one weekend to somewhere in Tennessee, with several different types of drugs on me and got arrested. The arresting officer said, "Son we are going to bury you under this jail." To which I responded, "I will be home before you are." He laughed. I showed him the business card the Narcotics Detective had given me. He gave him a call and one hour later they released me … with my car keys, but better yet, they gave me *all* my drugs back.

Eventually they wanted real information so I left and went to either Illinois to hang with my Amish friends or back to Florida. I am not sure which. Mass quantities of drugs will definitely distort one's memory.

Comedy or tragedy? Around nineteen seventy-seven, nineteen years old and quite often suicidal, when no one was around and the party was over, even if the beast had been fed and fed well, the darkness would settle in. I needed the pain to stop but no amount of drugs could dull it when I was alone.

One night everyone else had either gone home or passed out. I was alone and wide awake. I decided, 'tonight is the night.' No more drugs or alcohol and therefore I took what I could find … twenty seven arthritis pain formula pills. No sooner had I swallowed them that I realized it wasn't such a good idea. I called for an ambulance, gave them the address and told them what I had done. Before they could get there I changed my mind again and decided to hide. When they arrived I was in the field across the street. One of the paramedics went to the door and barely even knocked. He went back to the ambulance and they started to drive off! I was enraged! I ran them down and started beating on the side of the ambulance screaming at them, "Weren't you called for a suicide? What if I were dying inside there?" They stopped, opened the door and took me to the emergency room where they pumped my stomach. That set me up for some time with a shrink.

With the shrink I made a feeble attempt for awhile at trying to stop ... very feeble. I tried going to the bars carrying around an empty beer. That lasted for one night. The shrink asked me once if I would take Antabuse. I had no idea what that was so I asked. He said, "It is a pill I can give you that will make you violently ill if you drink while taking it." I laughed and said, "Hell no." He asked, "Why not?" I quickly responded, "What if I change my mind?" His time in my life was short lived.

I was given ten months in the County jail for my blue light specials at K–Mart. It was only considered a misdemeanor. I was in there with one of my dad's childhood friends and drinking buddies, Jiggs. He was my jail mentor. He schooled me on how to get by in jail. Not like I hadn't been there enough but this time I was doing time.

The social worker came down to the cells every Wednesday. She always singled out one person to spend her time with. Almost every time, that person got to leave soon after her visit. I finally asked Jiggs, "Who is she and what does she do?" A light suddenly came on for Jiggs, "Man, Johnnie we need to set you up an appointment with her. If you tell her you were selling that stuff to support your alcoholism she will get your time suspended and send you to alcohol treatment."

That is exactly what we did. When I met with Sandra I played up the alcoholism line really well (My denial had me believing that it was a con) and I was then sent to an alcohol treatment center with absolutely no intention of quitting. I had totally given up on even pretending there was any hope for me and so had all my family, maybe, even Jane Ann.

They all knew when I was being released, seventy miles away. No one would come to get me. I no longer had any friends. I had burned them all, one way or another. "Do unto them ..." had finally caught up with me. There was no one left to do unto.

I had two dollars in my pocket the day I got out of treatment. I walked out the door and across the street to the liquor store, bought a half a pint of rum and stole a half a pint of vodka. Once again I had no idea how dark things could really get. With my two little bottles of liquid courage I started hitchhiking home. Actually I went to my favorite bar.

I knew everyone there and they all knew me. There was no parade for my release. It was as if I had never been gone. There was an old guy at the bar who I had never seen there before. He was really drunk. Somehow I talked him into buying my drinks. In our conversation he mentioned he needed a truck. My truck had been sitting for five months. I told him it was for sale. In his drunken stupor he wanted to see it so I took that man down every back road there was to find the truck, knowing he would not be able to find his way back to get it. He gave me a two hundred dollar down payment, and that was the last time I ever saw him. Over the next few months I sold that truck four or five times. I always promised to deliver it, but of course, never did. I drove it myself. One guy was even making payments.

I wasn't even twenty four hours out of jail and treatment and I was back to my same old games. It was November in Kentucky and cold. I was living in an abandoned trailer on this old dirt road, with no electricity or water. Showers were a thing of the past. Periodically I would go to one of my grandmothers' houses or Jane Ann's and clean up. They would wash my clothes while I showered and I would put on something there while they dried.

One very cold morning I woke up from a long drunk in that trailer and decided that I was going to Florida. I had been told that Jackie was living in Sarasota. I had twelve dollars to my name and all my clothes were on my back. I may have had clothes scattered around between my grandmothers' houses and Jane Ann's but I didn't look back. I just left, with no goodbyes, nothing ... just one day I was gone.

Upon my arrival in Florida, the dark got even darker. All the while I was ripping and tearing in Kentucky there was one line that even I would not cross. The needle! I wouldn't allow myself to become a junkie. Once in Florida, I didn't even question it. It was presented to me and I never hesitated. Once I crossed that line there was no going back.

Jackie's boyfriend, Zack was the first one to 'get me off' with a needle. Three days after that first time I went back for more. Zack just looked at me and said, "No. I will not do that for you again. You have the itch in your eye more than anyone I have ever seen and I won't be the one to take you down that road." Zack was a biker, a junkie, a criminal but evidently he still had a heart. Either that or he was scared of Jackie!

Finding someone else to help me "shoot up" was not a difficult task. Almost everyone I had met so far was a junkie. It wasn't long before I was doing it myself. Not many would understand the adrenalin buzz that one gets from 'shooting up'. Without thinking about it there is an inner knowing that you have your life in your own hands. The ritual of getting everything ready was all a part of the allure of it.

I was not in a place where I could afford real dope. Therefore I learned how to make bathtub crank. This stuff was made out of nasal inhalers and … muriatic acid. Muriatic acid will burn a hole in concrete and I was cooking it until it crystallized and shooting it into my veins. It only cost about six dollars to make a gram. It wasn't even costing me that much; I was stealing the inhalers and a gallon jug of the acid would last for months. I could sell this stuff for sixty dollars a gram to the real junkies. They could not afford real dope either. The money from the sales gave me drinking and pot money.

The beast that lived within me had an insatiable appetite. The more I fed it the more it wanted. I was shooting up as much of that bathtub crank as I could make. It was literally non-stop. Along with the syringe and whatever I could get in it, I was constantly drinking, smoking pot and using anything else I could find. I was mixing drugs all the time. It was nothing for me to do crank and some kind of downers together.

One night I was doing green micro-dot acid; five of them. I had absolutely lost everything. I had one pair of pants, one shirt, a size nine blue flip flop and a size ten and a half red flip flop. The guys that I was hanging out with took me to this party. A really nice house, a big party and no one like me (a junkie).

All of a sudden there she stood; beautiful, blonde, tanned and laughing at my jokes. Lucy lived in that house. It was actually her party. She started giving me the tour. Me? Why would this beautiful woman even be talking to me? I didn't understand. She was dressed very nicely and had this really nice smile and an infectious laugh. I can safely say that I had on a pair of pants and a shirt that I had been wearing for days without being washed. My personal hygiene, to say the least, was lacking. And she liked me. Wow!

She said, "You have the sexiest accent I think I have ever heard." Suddenly it was like I had been born and raised in Alabama. My accent was already pretty thick but after that statement, it got *real* thick.

I spent the night with her. I did the best I could to be a gentleman. The next morning she was up before me. Evidently several others had crashed there too. When I strolled into the main room where everyone was gathered, she acted embarrassed that I had just come from her room. She acted like she didn't know me. I wasn't surprised. It hurt but I think I even expected it. I couldn't really blame her. I looked and probably smelled like death warmed over.

I just sauntered out the front door to leave and suddenly realized that I had no idea where I was. For the first time in a very long time I had to look at what I had become. I was this thing, just an existence, no clothes, no real shoes, no home and all alone.

I had met some Amish guys and had been partying with them for quite a while. I had actually gone to northern Illinois with them during part of the lost time. I have no clue where that falls in the time line. I had been staying with them, sleeping on their couch, in downtown Sarasota. When I left Lucy's house I somehow found my way back to their place.

The night I met Lucy was a Saturday. Somehow, someway when Monday came around I was sitting in the house with a beer and a joint and I looked up and there she was, standing in the door asking, "Do you guys know Fat Freddy?" Fat Freddy was my alias. No one in Florida even knew Johnnie Calloway, so that was how Lucy knew me. The one and only shirt that I owned even had Fat Freddy printed on the back. On the front was a picture of a monster, with the statement across the top, 'I'm the one your mother warned you about.'

'What the hell was she doing there?' And, 'What the hell did she want?' I did not remember stealing anything from her. That didn't mean I hadn't, I just didn't remember it if I had. I went to the door and asked, "Can I help you?" She said, "Yeah I was hoping we could hang out, maybe I can take you to dinner."

I still had on those same clothes. I was very high and drunk and this very pretty lady was here to take me to dinner. I said, "Sure." And off we went. After dinner she took me to her house, let me take a shower and had a change of clothes for me to put on. She moved me in with her that night! I was twenty-three at the time.

Just prior to meeting Lucy, I was staying wherever I could, mostly between the Amish guys' house and this girl named Chris' house. I had become a total slave to the syringe. I was constantly writing this very dark poetry. I wrote it on napkins, envelopes, business cards … anything would do.

Chris loved my poetry. Her life was pretty dark as well and she could relate to the pain I wrote about. One night Chris handed me a book and said, "Here Freddy, this is for you." I opened it and all the pages were blank. I snapped at her jokingly and said, "You think I can't read?" "No you idiot." She snapped back, "It is for your poems, you need to keep them."

That was in February, nineteen eighty-two. I know because I dated the poems and by some miracle I still have the book; just like the baby book. I am absolutely amazed that I have held on to them.

On the front page of the book I wrote:

"In this book is my explanation of myself. All my different moods are seen, my ups and my downs. I just have to explain ..."

The first poem: Friday Feb. fifth nineteen eighty two.

From one home to another
My life has been passed
Lost a friend then a brother
Been a small supporting cast

The lovers I lost
I made them all friends
But my heart it has cost
Few were true friends

I want to be gentle
I want to be good
Love the world just a little
If only I could

I've got to be rough
Seem to be mean
But you know I'm not tough
If the real me you've seen

Fat Freddy was the name I acquired upon coming to
Florida. Fat Freddy was a character in a comic book about
three hippies, The Fabulous Furry Freak Brothers. All three
were potheads and druggies. I was very heavy at the time and
Fat Freddy just fit for me.

After I met Lucy, everything changed. She took me to JC
Penny and bought me some clothes and some work boots. She
took me to a dentist to get my teeth cleaned. She insisted that
if I was going to stay with her I would have to get a job and
stop using a syringe. I did!

I got a job at a dairy farm east of Sarasota. Part of my pay was a mobile home to live in. Lucy would stay with me most of the time. I told her everything and she still stayed. A good portion of the poems I wrote in the book that Chris gave me were written for Lucy. I asked her to marry me. It had to be an act of God but she said, "Yes." I know all of her friends warned her not to. I know they all asked her what the hell she was thinking. But she still said "yes." I still do not understand why.

On the day we were to get married I got fired one hour before the ceremony. She was devastated. It should have been an omen for her. For me it was just another day in the life of Johnnie Calloway. We were supposed to move into the mobile home which came with my job, but now I had no job. We were newly married and we had no home.

I got so drunk and high on acid on our wedding day, I was of no use to her on our honeymoon. She hadn't a clue what she had just gotten herself into and I thought that as long as I didn't go back to the syringe, all would be well.

To try to appease her I got a job, then another job and another and another. I was really good at getting jobs. I just couldn't keep a job. She was living in hell. And I was the keeper of the key. I never put my hands on her in a hurtful way. The mental anguish and emotional hell I put her through may have been just as bad as if I had hit her.

My self-hatred was unimaginable. I wanted to be a husband, hell even a friend. Somehow she still seemed to love me. I was doing nothing to deserve her loyalty or her love. The beast was being fed alcohol and pot all day every day. But there was that gnawing unrelenting echo of the beast wanting its real desire, the syringe.

My mind started screaming at me, all the old tapes that were so ingrained in me. "He's just one of those Calloways",

"We're cursed", "Once a drunk always a drunk" (and now a junkie). And there was always the guilt of my mother, plus what I had put Jane Ann through and now Lucy ... not to mention everyone else that I had hurt. I gave in.

Once I went back to the syringe, it was like putting our marriage on a very fast paced merry go round. I would go on a junkie binge, she would threaten to leave, and I would settle down for a while. Then the cycle would start again. My settling down periods got shorter and shorter and her threats to leave got more sincere.

Typically a junkie hides because shooting drugs is not socially acceptable. I was no longer hiding. In fact, at one party, I sat right in the middle of the living room, shooting up, and announced to the entire group, "Don't ever do this. You won't ever be able to stop." I was screaming in agony for help and was totally convinced there was no help. I had tried treatment, church and just stopping. I hurt everyone and everything I touched. I only wanted one more thing ... to die. Suicide was not an option but overdosing was. My drug usage and my drinking became a serious death wish, using in proportions that should have killed anyone, but not me. Surviving it all seemed like punishment. I was angry with God for not letting me go.

I was no longer doing the bathtub crank. I was shooting real dope, cocaine. I no longer even tried to hold a job. The memory of how I got by with that with Lucy is gone. I do remember feeling incredibly beaten. The beast was eating me. It had won.

Thanksgiving nineteen eighty-four, now twenty- six years old, and my coke dealer fronted me one quarter ounce of coke, to be paid for on Monday. I sold all of it! I made two hundred dollars. I decided that dealing would be my vocation.

The weekend of December third, nineteen eighty-four was utter hell. I was literally trying to overdose. My dealer this time fronted me one half ounce of cocaine. I should have been able to make over five hundred dollars. I never sold the first line. As I was weighing the coke out to sell, I had the brilliant idea to test what I had cut. Oops! After the test all bets were off.

Of course I had other junkie friends (oxymoron: junkies don't make good friends). I bagged up all the coke and headed out to sell my goods. I went to this guy's house and we started shooting. I was doing one shot after the other in mass quantities. After each shot I would silently look to the ceiling and ask, "Was that one not big enough?" I didn't die so I took that as a "no". Then another, just bigger this time, same thing, still breathing. Each dose was bigger than the last and becoming more and more frequent. My junkie friend couldn't keep up. He really didn't even try even though I was giving it to him for free. He had a young baby boy. He finally said, "Freddy you cannot die here, I have a child in this house."

By this time I was already gone for a day and a half. I went to another junkie's house. I left my syringe at the first guy's house and the new guy only had a veterinarian's syringe. It had a point on it the size of a finishing nail. There was simply no way you could stick yourself without bleeding. I was still going at it with a fury and still asking God, "How much does it take?" More than anything else I wanted to die. I could no longer bear being with myself. I had *become* the beast. I was no longer using the drugs. The drugs were using me.

Lucy had been looking for me the entire time. She finally caught up. My friend went to the door after she rang the bell. Then he shouted, "Freddy, your old lady is here." Normally I would have covered up my arms so she wouldn't see what was going on. Now, I was beyond caring. I went to the door with both arms bleeding badly. She immediately started sobbing and shouted, "You're shooting dope." I responded, "No shit!" then followed with, "Please leave me. You do not deserve this." She turned and walked away, still sobbing. The spiral down to hell can be long and very grueling.

Soon after she was gone, this junkie friend echoed the thoughts of the friend before him. "You can't die here." I left.

Before Lucy, I had known this quadriplegic girl, Ruth Ann. I knew I could do anything at her house. I still had plenty of coke left. Of course I was also drinking and smoking pot while all this was going on. Alcohol and pot for me were like air and water; necessary for life.

Once at Ruth Ann's, I went right back to it as hard as ever, even more focused on dying. Ruth Ann was crying, "Freddy you have got to stop. Even you can't survive this." I just laughed and continued. Now I was basically begging God to let each shot be the last. No! He just wouldn't let me die. Eventually I ran out of coke ... still breathing.

Ruth Ann gave me two blue Valium and said, "Maybe this will help you sleep." I went to lie down on her couch, looked up at the ceiling and said, "Please just do not let me wake up." I eventually passed out. I 'came to' a few hours later, looked up at that same ceiling and said, "Fuck you. I ask you to do the whole world a favor and just take the breath from my body and you won't even do that for me. Fuck you."

I soon rushed home hoping to catch Lucy before she had a chance to follow my directions.

She was there! Maybe, just maybe there was hope. I knew that if she left me, I was done. When I walked in, her suitcases were at the front door and she was frantically moving about getting her stuff together. She was done. I couldn't blame her. I was consumed with guilt and remorse. I knew I needed help and I knew I needed her but I didn't think there was help for *me* in either case.

I begged her to stay. "Please give me one more chance. I will get help." I truly would have liked to believe there was help/hope for me. I was convinced though, that there was nothing that *could* help me. Part of the reason I was in this mess, I believed, was because God, Himself had given up on me long ago. Actually at that moment I still believed that my entire life had been God punishing me and I had just continually given him more reasons to punish me. And now, the worst of his punishment; He let me live.

I started making phone calls to treatment centers with Lucy right by my side. I was almost having a panic attack. I knew if Lucy left that I would go back to shooting the bathtub crank and die a slow and lonely death.

I had no faith whatsoever that there was help for someone like me. Everyone I called said, "No insurance, no help." One lady said, "There are meetings you can go to." I knew about the Twelve Step Programs from when I had gone to treatment in the past. I knew about my dad being taken to some of those meetings and coming home drunk. I did not believe they worked. When she told me about the meetings I responded, "You don't have meetings for a guy like me." Thinking my only problem was the coke, I was ready to give up the coke and the syringe, but alcohol and pot too? No way. She stated, with a chuckle, "Yes, we have meetings for people exactly like you."

Lucy was sitting right beside me while I was having the phone conversation. I could not maneuver my way out. So a meeting it was. It was Monday, December third, nineteen eighty four. At twenty six years old I went to my first Twelve Step meeting voluntarily that night.

And ... my life would never be the same.

CHAPTER 7

THE BEGINNING

I wanted Lucy to go with me to the Twelve Step meeting, so she could see I was serious. I really did not know myself how much I wanted to stop until I was at that first meeting.

It was a big group, thirty or forty people, all ages, all races, both sexes, well dressed folks and bums; all were welcome. With all my addictions I never smoked cigarettes. The meeting broke off into two meetings; smokers and non-smokers. I took Lucy with me to the non-smokers meeting. There was Lucy, myself, and seven others in that little room.

There was a lot of reading in the beginning. Then the floor was opened up for discussion. The first guy had gotten clean and sober and found Jesus. He started quoting scripture and I immediately related it to church and thought to myself, 'Same old stuff and it will never work for me. I just can't get good enough fast enough.' The second guy was going through a divorce and was saying, "That fucking bitch this and that fucking bitch that." And no one told him he couldn't cuss, no one told him to shut up. They just let him speak his mind. I breathed and thought, 'I just might be able to do this.'

I could not complete a sentence without the f-bomb in it. If they had told me I couldn't cuss I probably wouldn't have gone back. What I got from that interaction was, 'There are no rules here.'

They shared about things I thought only I had done, feelings I thought only I had and ... they laughed, that real gut-felt belly laugh that stays with you awhile. I wanted that. Whatever it was they had, I wanted it.

They shared about how their lives were changing, how they had been to jail, lost their families, their jobs, how their kids wouldn't talk to them and that they had no friends left. But now, they had their lives back, they had found new jobs, their kids were talking to them, their parents had allowed them back in the house and things seemed to be coming together for them. This all couldn't have been an act just for me. It certainly did speak to my life. The only thing left for me was Lucy and she was there only by a shoestring. She still hadn't unpacked her bags.

The people at the meeting told me about working some steps, going to ninety meetings in ninety days, getting a sponsor and having a higher power. They called it higher power but I knew they were talking about God. I did not know how that was going to work. He had been out to get me my whole life and now they said if I was going to stop using I was going to need a higher power in my life. For me, that was a stretch. They also said that this wasn't just about hard drugs. I was going to have to stop using all mood altering drugs. I wasn't sure about the alcohol and the pot ... that might be more than I was willing to give up.

The thing that stuck with me the most was, they said, "If you want to stop using you have to get honest." I had always wanted more than anything else to be honest. As a boy, lying all the time, I would actually fantasize about being honest. I told someone as a child (not sure what age) "life would be so much easier if God hadn't made lying an option." I had always wanted to be one of the good guys with the white hat. My heroes were The Rifleman, Marshall Dillon, The Cartwrights; all those white-hat-wearing guys. I couldn't get a white hat to fit my head to save my life and the thing that kept it most from fitting was my lack of honesty. I lied all the time about things that didn't even matter. And they were telling me that honesty was the only thing that would get and keep me clean.

I had no idea how I was going to pull this off but they told me that they had been just like me and now they were good people. They weren't drinking, drugging, stealing or lying and their lives were getting better, one day at a time. The miracle was I believed them.

My doubt was I just wasn't sure I could do this. I didn't think they knew about the Calloway curse. I did know they weren't aware that I killed my mom. Yes, even though I was a grown man that child within me still held onto that guilt. They also said, "Keep coming back" and didn't preface it with "Don't you ever!"

They gave me a book about the Twelve Steps. I left that first meeting with the overwhelming sensation of being home. I do not know if I had ever felt that before but I felt it then. My soul breathed a sigh of relief. And for the first time in a long time there was hope.

I took that book home and started to read it. As I read it, I felt the need to look over my shoulder and see who had been watching. I thought, 'Someone had been reading my mail.' It was me to a tee. I had never read anything that so perfectly described me. I had never known hope like I did then. Others had already blazed a trail for me. I wasn't the only one.

All of a sudden everything was new.

For every other thing I had ever done to try to find help, I had looked for reasons why it wouldn't work. This time was truly different. I looked for reasons why I *could* be helped, how I *could* fit in. I did not have to look far. I was being helped already, and I did fit in. This was where I belonged.

They told me to attend ninety meetings in ninety days. I committed myself to doing just that. They also said to do the Twelve Steps.

The Twelve Steps

1. We admitted that we were powerless over our addiction, that our lives had become unmanageable.
2. We came to believe that a power greater than ourselves could restore us to sanity.
3. We made a decision to turn our lives over to the care of God as we understood Him.
4. We made a searching and fearless moral inventory of ourselves.
5. We admitted to God, to ourselves, and another human being the exact nature of our wrongs.
6. We were entirely ready to have God remove all these defects of character.
7. We humbly asked Him to remove our shortcomings.
8. We made a list of all persons we had harmed, and became willing to make amends to them all.
9. We made direct amends to such people wherever possible, except when to do so would injure them or others.
10. We continued to take personal inventory and when we were wrong promptly admitted it.

11. We sought through prayer and meditation to improve our conscious contact with God as we understood Him, praying only for knowledge of His will for us and the power to carry that out.
12. Having had a spiritual awakening as a result of these steps, we tried to carry this message to addicts, and to practice these principles in all our affairs.

Admitting I was powerless was easy. How many times had I told Lucy, "I will bring my check home tonight. I won't stop at the bar"? Only to 'come to' later in our bed, with her standing over me asking, "What happened to your check?" The hundreds of times that I had promised myself, 'I'm only going to play one game of pool.' All the times I had gone to either of my grandmothers' houses, fully intending to tell them how much I appreciated all they had done for me, only to leave with something of value in my pocket so I could feed the beast. I could not deny any longer all the emotional devastation I had left in my wake. Here, with these people in the Twelve Step meetings, I had to admit complete defeat. The beast had beaten me. Admitting and accepting that was actually a relief.

They said the only way to win was to surrender. That whole idea just boggled my mind. Boggling my mind at that time was not a difficult task.

Was my life unmanageable? Again I could not deny the facts even if I had wanted to. I absolutely could not follow through with any commitment. Promises were meaningless. If I did have a job and a party was presented to me, the job had to wait or I would quit.

One day on a job it started raining and I just needed to go to the bar and play pool. I told my foreman that I needed to leave. He asked what was up. Not wanting to bother myself by coming up with a lie, I said, "It's raining." He said, "We're working inside! You're kidding right?" "Nope," I said, "I got to go." He sighed and asked, "Are you coming in tomorrow?" "Can I?" I responded. If he had said "no" I would have quit. Yes! My life was unmanageable.

I wanted more than anything to fit in with the guys at the meetings. Even if I hadn't believed I was an addict/alcoholic I would have lied and said I was. But I didn't need to lie.

For the first time my desire to be the best at something was paying off. I went at the steps like I was trying to put out a fire. I guess I was. After my fourth meeting I walked up to this guy. I didn't even know his name, but I had heard him share at every meeting, and I asked, "Could you help me with my fourth step?" His response, "Hello I am Tim. Who are you?" "I am Johnnie; I want to do my fourth step." "What about the other three?" he asked. After a little conversation he suggested that I do the other three first and he said something about them being in order for a reason.

I was just so anxious to have someone listen to the insanity of my life. I had all this built up inside me and it was going to explode. At the Boys' Camp I had learned the importance of sharing the pain. I needed to let it go.

I needed a guide to help me with the steps. Everyone was telling me I was trying to go too fast and that I should slow down. They had told me that the steps would make me better. I felt that I had waited for a long time to get better I didn't want to wait any longer.

My thought was, 'If I go to the doctor for a cold and he writes me a prescription, I wouldn't go buy the medicine, get home and ask when he wanted me to take it. Because the answer would always be that you follow the directions when you are truly ready to get better.' I was ready and I wanted it yesterday.

I just kept asking for someone to help me with the steps until I found a guy who said he would. Bill made my first trip through the steps simple. He told me to follow the directions as they are laid out in the book for the fourth step. "We made a searching and fearless moral inventory of ourselves."

I therefore made a list of the people I resented. How they affected me and a list of my fears. What I did was to write down all the harm that had been done to me. It was an extensive list. Poor Bill, I know he had no idea what he had signed up to listen to but listen he did, for at least two and a half hours.

It began like this: He asked, "Can you use drugs or alcohol successfully?" A resounding "No," was my response. "When you use drugs or alcohol are you managing your life?" "No," I said. "Okay, that is the first step."

"Do you believe there is a power greater than you that can restore you to sanity?" was his next question. "I am not sure. I do believe in you guys though," I said. In an incredible gentleness he said, "That is good enough for now. We can work on that. And that is step two."

"Are you willing to turn your will and your life over to the care of the God of your understanding?" Almost crying now, I quietly said, "I am willing to try but I am not sure I believe." We then said Bill's version of the third step prayer together. "God I offer myself to you to build with me and do with me as You will. Relieve me of the bondage of self that I may better do Your will. Take away my difficulties that victory over them may bear witness to those I would help of Your Power, Your Love, and Your Way of life. May I do Your will always!"

After the prayer, he chuckled as he said to me, "You have always believed in a power greater than you. You always believed drugs and alcohol would give you the things you felt you were lacking; courage to talk to the girl, you believed they could make you taller, more handsome, and give you the strength to not walk away from a fight. You have put all your faith in drugs and alcohol. And ... for a time they worked. Then that god turned against you and started destroying your soul. It is now time for you to choose a God that will work *for* not *against* you. Can you try to trust me on this?" Meekly I stated, "Yes I will try."

"Now let's do step four." "We made a searching and fearless moral inventory of ourselves". Finally he had me read what I had written. I was so ready for this. As I was reading it to him he was writing stuff down on a little note pad he had brought with him. I actually thought to myself, 'I knew he was going to be impressed but I never thought about him writing it down.'

In the book, the guide for the fourth step states, "On our grudge list we set opposite each name, our injuries. Was it our self esteem, our security, our ambitions, our personal, or sex relations, which had been interfered with?"

I'm resentful at	The Cause	Affects my:
Mr. Brown	His attention to my wife	Sex relations
		Self –esteem (fear)
	Told my wife about my mistress	Sex relations
		Self –esteem (fear)

I followed those directions as closely as I possibly could. I truly wanted the program to work. My list of resentments covered several pages. Pretty much, if I had known you I resented you. My mind was still trapped in the mind of that child. Either you had harmed me or you could have rescued me and you didn't. I was torn in almost every area as to whether I was responsible or a victim.The confusion was intense. There were several effects to each resentment.

The directions in the book also suggested we put our fears on paper. I was seriously afraid of almost everything. I was very afraid I would drink again. I was afraid of never having money, of having money, of Lucy leaving me, Lucy staying, not having a job, having a job. Bill just sat and listened and jotted down a note here and there with an occasional, "Damn man! That had to suck." or some statement about how he could relate. Mostly he just listened. There was a tear when I talked about my guilt for my mom and I could tell he was really trying to hold it back.

I told him everything! Everything that had been done to me and everything I had done. It felt like a good hot shower after a long day of working in the sun. My soul sighed. I was so relieved. We chatted for a bit after I finished the reading. Bill shared with me all the ways he could relate, mostly with the things I had done. The truth is he couldn't relate very well to my childhood. I could tell he felt a degree of sadness for me as a child.

"Now you are ready for steps six and seven." Six: "Were entirely ready to have God remove all these defects of character." Seven: "Humbly asked Him to remove our shortcomings." After the brief chat and the reading of those two steps, he pushed his notes in my direction and said, "Here is the list of your character defects and shortcomings that I noticed. Don't worry, there are more. You will spend the rest of your life working on your defects and shortcomings."

As for step eight: "Made a list of all persons we had harmed, and became willing to make amends to them all."Again, after we read the step he interjected, "You will find most of your list on your fourth step. You have more than likely in some way screwed everyone you resented. Your entire list will not be there. You have also screwed some innocent bystanders. Look thoroughly over your resentment list for those you have harmed and add the rest, trying not to think about the next step."

Step nine: we read, "Made direct amends to such people wherever possible except when to do so would injure them or others." With a stronger sense of sincerity than before he said with a conviction, "The freedom from your past will be directly contingent on your willingness to do this step. All the sooner you clean up your past the more free you will be to step into a new tomorrow." This seemed to have more meaning to him than anything else we had covered. I took it to heart.

As we read step ten together, Bill was smiling, "Continued to take personal inventory and when we were wrong promptly admitted it." Almost laughing now, he said with a great joy, "Doing this step thoroughly will help you to not have to do this shit again." I laughed with him.

After our little laugh about step ten, without reading the steps, Bill said, "Step eleven you need to practice every day. It will bring you peace and serenity ... words that are foreign to you and may even frighten you. And step twelve will give all the insanity you have lived through a purpose. Your past can become your greatest asset to helping others if you don't regret it to the point of closing the door on it."

Then we read Step Eleven: "Sought through prayer and meditation to improve our conscious contact with God as we understood Him, praying only for knowledge of His will for us and the power to carry that out." And Step Twelve: "Having had a spiritual awakening as the result of these steps, we tried to carry this message to alcoholics, and to practice these principles in all our affairs."

I will be forever indebted to Bill and his simplistic approach to The Twelve Steps of recovery. There are literally hundreds of ways to do these steps. I have seen it over and over. If a person truly wants to recover, God will direct them to the right person, at the right time, and lead them in a way that works for them. As we say in the meetings 'There is a wrench for every nut in here.' God led me to the right wrench. He will, and has done it for countless others.

The Twelve Steps were only the beginning.

CHAPTER 8

THE WORK

1. Honesty

The steps had given me a foundation upon which I could build a *new* house. But there was still so much more for me to do. There is the old adage, "If you walked into the woods for a year, you can't turn around and walk out in a week." I had walked into the woods my entire life. After the first round with The Twelve Steps at least I had turned around and started back out.

In all Twelve Step Programs, it is suggested to get a sponsor; one who is basically a guide through the steps and a mentor on how to use the principles of those steps in your daily life. We suggest finding someone who has what you want. I hadn't a clue what I wanted, I just knew I wanted to be a better man than I was.

I was going to meetings every day. After I discovered there were Twelve Step noon meetings, sometimes I went twice a day. That noon meeting was held in a clubhouse. I did not know where it was and wasn't sure I believed there was a noon meeting. I got the number to the club, (remember my brain was still fried) which I called and a gentleman named Lloyd answered. He said, "This is the 12 step club." I asked, "Do you have a noon meeting?" "Yep,"Lloyd responded. Then in all my newly recovering brilliance I asked, "What time is that meeting?" There was a pause before Lloyd answered, "We try to have that *noon* meeting around twelve o' clock." Lloyd and I had our first of many laughs together, most at my expense.

There was a guy, Ed, who started calling me every Sunday, asking if I would like to go deep sea fishing. I would say, "No, I can't afford it." He always offered to pay. He was really puzzling the hell out of me. I could not imagine what he was up to or what he wanted. He was starting to irritate me and one Sunday I volleyed, "What do you want?" He snickered, as he often did/does and quickly asked, "What do you have?" The answer was "nothing." I did not have anything for him to be after. We weren't doing drugs or drinking so he couldn't be after my dope. I didn't have a job or any money, so he couldn't be after that. I was befuddled. He asked, "Did it ever occur to you, that I may just like your company?" My thoughts were, "Hell no! And, why would you?" No one had ever just wanted to hang out with me without a payoff.

Ed had everything I thought I wanted in a sponsor. He was popular in our groups. He had a pretty wife, his own business, his own house, TOOLS, and two baby boys (Not what they meant in how to choose a sponsor). Fortunately Ed had all the stuff I wanted and didn't know I wanted; integrity, honesty, a sense of humor and a relationship with a God of his understanding.

I was obsessed with the honesty concept. I was telling the truth when sometimes I would have been better off to just hush. Lying by omission is still lying but there is no need to be brutal.

Lucy and I did not have our rent money that first month after I quit using. We had called her parents and asked for some help. They came up to Sarasota from Naples for a visit. We told them that I had a problem with alcohol but I was going to meetings. They were very understanding and said they would help. I felt like we were lying. That scared me. I was going to meetings but our money problem was over cocaine not alcohol. They were to come back over the next Sunday and take us to church, then come over for lunch and let us have the money. The idea that we were lying and I would drink if I lied was weighing heavily on me. We went to church and I could not bear the lie. I sat in that church, the whole time looking at Jesus on the cross and thinking about how badly I wanted to do the right thing. I knew that if they knew the problem was coke and not alcohol they would not let us have any money. On the way home from church I told Lucy that I had to tell them the truth. She freaked out. I tried to explain to her that I really wanted to straighten my life out and the guys at the meetings said I *must* get honest or use again. She didn't want to hear it. I told them the truth. They said "No money for the druggie." They did not speak to their daughter for a very long time after that. I had so much to learn.

About three months into my recovery I got a job. One afternoon I came home from work and Lucy was all excited about some shopping she had done. I was happy for her because she hadn't done that in some time and she deserved it. While I had been ripping and tearing she had maintained a job and kept the bills paid. So actually, *ecstatic* would describe her mood. She came into the living room all bubbly and cheery and styling her new jeans, asking, "Honey do these jeans make my butt look big?" Without even thinking, I said, "Those jeans don't have a thing to do with it." I should have lied. I did not want to take that moment from her. But I was very seriously afraid that if I lied about anything I would drink and drug. When I told Ed, after his belly laugh, he just said, "You might want to back off the honesty a bit. That one is going to cost you for awhile."

One day I was riding home from work with two guys. I was sitting in the back seat, while they smoked a joint and drank beer in the front. I was trying to be involved, but without the beer or the joint. One of them told a story about his dog being in a dog fight. I really wanted to be included and did what I had done so many times in the past. I told a story I had fabricated many years ago about a dog I had that killed another dog in a fight. The only truth of it was I did have the dog.

Once I told the story I realized I had lied. I was actually panic stricken. I had been convinced that to lie was to use again. I jumped back up between them and almost screamed, "That story I just told was all a lie, I made it up. In my group they told me that if I lie I will drink again. I really do not want to drink. I must tell the truth. That story never happened." We were still a good thirty minutes from home. There was not another word spoken the rest of the way.

2. TRUST

I had never trusted anyone in my entire life. There were a few that I could have but I didn't know how. The fear of trusting was bigger than I was. Everyone that I had trusted had turned on me except Jane Ann and Jackie; although with Jackie, the straight razor to the throat was a little scary. But everyone else was suspect.

Therefore, I didn't understand why I trusted Ed the way I did. I intuitively just knew I could. I not only believed what he said but also who he was and I felt he had my best interest at heart. Looking back, he said things to me that I really needed to hear but some of them were difficult. I often thought if he had said some of those things to me in a bar, we would have been in a fight. Somehow I knew he only said them to help me.

Once, after we had been to a meeting and the topic was 'trust', I asked him when I would be able to trust like they could. He simply said, "When you quit lying." I had already stopped lying but I hadn't forgiven myself for who I had been. And I most certainly didn't trust that the new me was for real.

I had wanted forever to just tell the truth. Ed made that possible. I could tell him everything and he still wanted to hang out with me. I didn't have to embellish things for him ... just the bare truth.

When I went for job interviews I told the bosses the truth. It is amazing how many people are willing to help when you tell the truth. I would get the job even after I told them my job history. Unfortunately I got to try that out a lot. My first year clean and sober I had fourteen jobs. I was even telling them the truth about the jobs I had just lost. I think they could sense I was being honest and they were willing to help me.

Even though I had already been through the Twelve Steps, as time passed Ed got to hear my entire story. "Johnnie, buddy, you have got some things going on for you that the Twelve Steps alone are not going to help. You are going to need some outside help."

Ed said it, so it must be so. I have often thought that initially when I did my Third Step, as a result of my not trusting God, my Third Step actually went like this: 'I turn my will and my life over to the care of *Ed* as I understand him.' I did practically everything he suggested. I was one of the fortunate ones. He could actually be trusted. Also the God (that I didn't trust) was saying things through him that I interpreted the way I needed to hear them.

I learned through Ed that in order to trust you must become trustworthy. It is really difficult to know you are a liar and not think everyone else is also. As I watched others in the meetings that had earned the trust of others I wanted to be trusted even more. I cherished the idea of being respected the way I had been at the Boys' Camp.

3. Challenges

Lucy and I were starting to have difficulties. She didn't like me going to meetings every night. She said I might as well be out drinking because I wasn't home anyway. She became jealous of my new friends. After the meetings every night some of the group would go for coffee. I totally absorbed myself with my new life.

Lucy wanted no part of it. She thought "those" people were sick. We were, but as a whole we were getting better. I knew that without these new friends I would drink and therefore would not be of any use to Lucy anyway.

It didn't help that she got a new job in an office. Suddenly I was just a construction worker. It was what I did and I was good at it. Lucy had higher aspirations. It was fine for her. Her attitude about me though seemed to be even worse than it was when I was a bum and wouldn't work. I could not keep a job but I always had a job; each job paying me more than the job before.

My self esteem was growing, I was feeling that I was a part of society and I wanted now to be a part of our family decisions. *I was alive!* Lucy didn't know how to handle the new me. She had always made all the decisions and I hadn't cared. The truth is I didn't want to be bothered with it before. Lucy lost control of me when I entered the Twelve Steps.

Ed had asked me shortly after we became friends, "Why did you come to your first meeting?" I responded, "Lucy doesn't like me drunk." After we started having trouble he asked, "What's going on with you and Lucy?" to which I replied, "Lucy doesn't like me sober." He laughed, "Maybe you need to consider, Lucy just doesn't like *you*. At least she may not like who you really are."

Lucy and I started talking about divorce. It wasn't helping me that the meetings were full of beautiful young girls that were paying me a lot of attention and simultaneously understood my *need* for the meetings and the fellowship I found in them.

It was such a weird time for me. I was totally aware that I had only come to that first meeting to calm Lucy down and get her to unpack. And now, there I was ready and willing to let her go for my recovery. I didn't just want to stop drinking and drugging I wanted to become the man that I knew my mother would still want me to be. With the help of the Twelve Steps I actually believed I could be that man.

What was I to do about Lucy? I burned Ed's phone up every day. We talked and talked. Lucy didn't want any part of what I had to do to grow up. When you get right down to it, that is what the Twelve Steps are really all about, "growing up". I was twenty seven years old with the mind of a fourteen year old kid. She wanted me to change but not this way.

We split up. It was inevitable. I hadn't actually followed Ed's advice about outside help until the split with Lucy. I hadn't a clue all the tentacles of dysfunction that were hanging off me. With our separation the real work began.

The Twelve Steps were the easy part. It was on the rest of my insanity, that the work was to take place. After the split with Lucy I was almost cocky about it. I moved in with a friend from the meetings. Lucy called me every day for two weeks begging me to come home. I would flippantly respond with, "You need to move on. I have done you a favor." She would hang up crying.

I am not proud of this but part of me was enjoying it. I had never had anyone cry over me. In my twisted little way it felt good. I had always been the one doing the crying. One night Lucy didn't call. I called her just to see how she was doing. When she answered she was in a great mood. I asked, "How are you?" The question was met with an immediate, "I am doing great! You were right! You did do me a favor."

I freaked out! I told her I would be right there. "No, that is okay I am going out with the girls." What I realized, that was so difficult to face, was that it was quite alright for me to not want her but it wasn't even a little bit okay for her to not want me.

When I would call Ed to talk to him about the things that were going on with us, I would start off with "She ... ". He always said, "She didn't call me so I can't help her. You, however, did call me, so let's talk about you and maybe I can help." He literally forced me to look at my part in all of it.

I was learning to face myself, to see how manipulative I could be and how much I played the victim. Facing and trying to change these things were the real challenges of recovery and growing up.

The therapist I acquired said, "You are only responsible for one hundred percent of your fifty percent in any relationship." All my life I had taken responsibility for things that weren't my responsibility; my Mom's death, my Dad's alcoholism, the anger in my family. I had taken responsibility for it all, except what truly was mine. I blamed everything that was mine on everyone else. Sorting out what was mine and what was someone else's after I got clean was most definitely a tall order.

Lucy stuck with the idea that I had done her a favor and moved on with her life. We were divorced the day before Thanksgiving, nineteen eighty five. I was twenty seven. Throughout Thanksgiving and Christmas the topics for discussion at meetings are commonly on 'gratitude'.

We were divorced at eleven o'clock so I made it to the noon meeting at the clubhouse. Someone brought up gratitude as the topic. I had just been divorced less than an hour before the meeting and was not in a particularly grateful mood. I managed to express my displeasure with the topic stating that I had nothing to be grateful for. An older gentleman that had befriended me spoke asked, "Johnnie, where are your in-laws having Thanksgiving dinner tomorrow?" Before I could answer he spoke again, "I bet it won't be with you." One of the older ladies interjected, "There is always a silver lining with every dark cloud." The whole room laughed out loud and I laughed with them. One of the most healing tools in recovery is laughter. Learning to laugh at myself and letting go of the seriousness was vital.

With the loss of Lucy, even though I was the one that left, the gut wrenching pain of abandonment returned. My stomach was in knots, I cried all the time and I was on a mad hunt for some female to fix me. Internally I was still crying for and looking for my mom.

My therapist said I was needy. When she said I was needy I felt sick inside like I was going to throw up. It just felt pathetic. I felt like this thing to be pitied. I felt incredibly small and humiliated.

Going through the break-up and divorce with Lucy, I almost drank twice. Once my car had broken down and I had to hitchhike home. Ed, his wife (Sue), and their two sons passed me on the road. They didn't even slow down. I was pissed. I was only one mile from what had been my favorite drinking place, Club Mary's, the topless bar where Jackie had worked. When Ed and Sue passed me I thought, 'Fuck it. Same old shit. Talk all that flowery talk in the meetings and get out here in the real world and this is who they are; won't even give a guy a ride.'

I went straight to Club Mary's, walked in sat at the bar and ordered a double bourbon and coke. The barmaid on shift said, "No Johnnie not here. You have done too good for too long and if you are going to mess up, it will have to be somewhere else." She had served me literally hundreds of drinks and now? Nothing. Her response woke me up. I realized what I was doing and freaked out. In the meetings we give our phone numbers out so when we get in trouble we can call on someone to help. I had a whole phone book in my pocket full of numbers. I called them all. No one was home. We also have a hotline number. I called it. The way it works is that you call the hotline and they take a number so someone can call you back. I had to leave the number for Club Mary's.

A few minutes later the phone rang and the bartender answered, "Club Mary's." She called me to the phone. By this time, after going to meetings everyday for over a year, I had become pretty popular in the program. When I got to the phone, what I heard was, "Johnnie?" I meekly responded, "Yes." Stephanie shrieked, "Program Johnnie?" "Yes." I said. "You haven't?" She blurted out. Almost crying now I said, "No not yet. Please come get me."

She was there in less than ten minutes. She drove me around for what seemed like forever just letting me ramble and cry. I will be forever indebted to her for that. All I can do now is try to pass it on to whoever is next. That is how the Twelve Step fellowships work. Whatever is given, you just pass it on to the next one in line. It is a debt that I will never be able to fully repay.

Going over my life with a therapist and revisiting all the hurt, while simultaneously feeling it as the result of the divorce, was hell. I had already gone through the steps, I was doing everything they were telling me I needed to do and I was coming apart inside.

Ed had been right! There were things in my life that the Twelve Steps alone weren't going to fix. And not even therapy was enough. I screamed in silence once again for help. I needed to have a closer relationship with and a better understanding of my God.

Way back in the beginning when I was really ready to do my Third Step (made a decision to turn our will and our lives over to the care of God as we understood Him), Ed had told me two things. "Since you don't have a God of your understanding, you get to make it up however you want it to be. When you say your prayers to Him, be honest with Him." The other thing he said after listening to me pontificate about all my ideas about a God I knew nothing about was, "It might behoove you to be open to the idea that perhaps everything that you think you know about God could be wrong." I don't think he had any idea what he had opened up for me.

My first honest prayer was "God, I do not know who you are, what you are or how you do what they say you do, but they are telling me that if I turn to you for help, I will change. I trust them when they say I can trust You. Please help me."

My life started changing almost immediately ... on my job if I only worked six hours I only turned six in; with Lucy, if I was late because I stood around talking after the meeting too long that is exactly what I told her... no made up stories. I began to feel like I belonged on this planet and it was no longer my place to be punished.

I believe today that God knows my heart. I do not need to know the right words. He knew that I *wanted* to know Him better. He heard the prayer of my heart pleading for a better understanding.

When I was twenty eight or twenty nine years old, clean and sober for a little over one and a half years, my friend Deborah was demonstrating a sense of calm and peace that intrigued me. I wanted to be around her all the time. I wasn't attracted to her physically, didn't want her to be my girlfriend but it just felt good to be around her.

One day Deborah's roommate had borrowed her car, put a ding in it, brought it back to the house and never told her about the accident. I was furious for Deborah but she was totally at peace with it. She was very understanding and forgiving. I told Deborah she was crazy but I also respected her for that ability. I asked, "How the hell do you do that?" She sighed a big sigh of relief and said, "I thought you would never ask."

She told me about these classes she was going to, 'A Course in Miracles'. It sounded a bit 'out there' to me but I wanted to know more about God. And Deborah had said that A Course in Miracles was all about God.

In my first ACIM class the lady in the front of the class was full of life, smiling, laughing, almost child-like and filled the room with joy. She had us all introduce ourselves. There were a few people in the class that I knew from the Twelve Step meetings. A couple of them I didn't really like.

After the introductions, Callie (the teacher) led us on a guided visualization. I had never experienced anything like that before. It was a spiritual experience. When she finished and had us open our eyes, the whole world was new again.

Those people that I didn't like suddenly were okay. I gave them pardon.

The class was now open for discussion. Everyone was sharing about these miracles that were happening in their lives. Once again, just like my first Twelve Step meeting, I felt I was home.

CHAPTER 9

THE COURSE

I was excited again about life. There were still issues to deal with but there was a new sense of hope. The God of my understanding was revealing Himself to me in these ACIM classes. The traditional way of believing about Him had not worked for me. A Course in Miracles was giving me an understanding that was working for me. My prior attempts had left me wanting.

While I was living with Jane Ann and going to church all the time, I truly wanted to believe that God loved me. For a short time I had tried to believe but I had questions and I needed answers.

We had a preacher, Brother Jones and I loved him. He was a younger man and he still understood the challenges that a teenager was up against. He befriended me. He took time with me to try and answer my questions. But even he often said to me, "That is just the way it is." That just never suited me. I could not understand a God that would leave me in question. There *had* to be answers.

One Sunday Brother Jones held us over, preaching about God's unconditional Love for us. I was so inspired and filled with the Spirit. I was Brother Jones' pet project. He cared about me and that was real. Often on the way out the door as he stood and shook everyone's hand, he would ask me how I felt about the service. I shared how inspired I was by the service. I was elated that God loved me unconditionally!

The very next Sunday we were held over, being taught how we were going to die and go to Hell if we didn't go to Africa and witness to those ignorant (his words) people. The wind was just let out of my sails. I was seriously depressed by this. It was a total contradiction to the message of just one Sunday earlier. I was seriously hoping Brother Jones would not ask me about the service. I was always honest with Brother Jones. He had been like Mr. Richards, my English teacher. He knew me. On the way out the door, he asked, "Johnnie boy, what did you think of today's service?" I tried to avoid the question. He would not allow it. He insisted on an answer.

"I was really hoping you wouldn't ask me today Brother Jones." He quickly responded, "Why son?" I sheepishly with my head bowed said, "Today's service was a complete contradiction of last Sunday's service." He was shocked. "What do you mean a contradiction?" Now the whole line of people who were trying to just get to their dinner were being held up by my confusion. So I lifted up my head and looking into his eyes said, "I don't care how you color it, Brother Jones, when you say, 'if you don't do this then this will happen', that is a condition. You can have it one way or the other He either loves us unconditionally or He loves us conditionally. You can't have it both ways."

He and I had several conversations about God after that. The best I ever got was, "You just have to accept it for what it is." I couldn't accept it then and I can't now. Soon after the two conflicting Sundays I started finding reasons to miss church.

Then later Callie, the ACIM teacher, became my therapist. I was getting answers to the questions I had asked for so long through A Course in Miracles. I was coming to have a God of *my* understanding.

As a child being rescued by a Good Samaritan and taken to church, I would hear, "Only a few are chosen." That statement made me very angry. I couldn't understand why I wasn't chosen. I wanted to be. Callie shared with me that ACIM says, "All are chosen and only a few choose to listen." I was so relieved with that information. Now it was my choice. God hadn't excluded me from His team, I had. It just seemed more loving to me.

After Callie and A Course in Miracles entered my life, the 'open mind' that Ed had coached me in the direction of began to have real value. I was seriously questioning everything that I had previously believed about God.

Another of the teachings that Callie shared with me from ACIM: "Vengeance is Mine, sayeth the Lord" does not mean God will be vengeful towards me. It means He will take the vengeance from my heart because it has no place there. I needed evidence of God's Love, not more reasons to be afraid of Him. It just seemed to make sense to me that if He were going to be vengeful for me against my Dad then He would also be vengeful to me for others that I had offended. I needed and wanted to know that he could/would forgive me. Another of the ACIM teachings that comforted me was, "You need not ask God for forgiveness, for God has never condemned you."

As my therapist, Callie was teaching me about forgiveness using the principles of A Course in Miracles and Twelve Steps. I found the principles of ACIM and the Twelve Steps are almost identical. She learned about my guilt over my Mother's death. I trusted Callie immediately, just as I had Ed. She offered me ideas for healing my brokenness that I would have scoffed at before. Between Ed helping me to open my mind and my trust in Callie, God was opening big doors for me.

After I explained to her how I had walked away from my mom's request for a kiss, she shared with me, "The mind does not know the difference between real and make believe. If you will trust me I think I can help you forgive yourself for what you did not do."

What happened next was one more major turning point for me. Through a process of guided visualization, Callie led me back to that hospital room. We envisioned the smell, the color, the energy and what it was like to be that little boy. For those few minutes I *was* that boy again. I could feel the confusion, the dread and the disappointment that I had felt so many years ago as that little child. I was truly there with my mom.

In the visualization, Callie described my mom perfectly and had her say to me, "Come give Momma a kiss goodbye." I was getting a second chance and I was reliving the whole scene. This time I could do what I would have done the first time, had I only known what goodbye meant and that goodbye in this case meant forever. This time I responded to her request by crawling up on that bed, snuggling with my mom and giving her a kiss, and I kissed her right on that sore. Also in the visualization, Callie had me just lay there with my Mom for awhile and be held by her. Then and only then could I truly let her go, it was finally time. The weight of the world had just been lifted off my shoulders and a new freedom was opening up to me.

After that experience I used this healing technique to mend many wounds from my past. I discovered the truth in the words, "It's never too late to have a happy childhood."

A Course in Miracles and the Twelve Steps combined, were a perfect blend for me. ACIM was giving me the understanding and faith in a God of my understanding and the Twelve Steps were giving me a guide and a support group for the practical application of the principles that both teach.

I was simultaneously living with one foot in heaven and the other still in hell. I was grateful beyond words for what I was learning but the application of what I was learning was like shedding skin. Everything that I had ever believed about anything was suspect. Not just about God, but also relationships, work ethic, friends, money... you name it, I was trying to become a man and it was not easy. I had been in a man's body with the mind and the heart of a boy for my entire adult life.

My instincts were all self-serving, manipulative and deceitful. Early on Ed had told me in a conversation about *ninety meetings in ninety days* and the importance of the steps. "Yes the steps and the meetings are very important but just as important is doing and being different." "Huh?" I responded. He continued, "If you continue to do what you have always done you will always get what you always got, so whatever your first instinct is to anything, try something else." Unlearning instincts that were deeply embedded in my being was to say the least, a daunting task. Learning to slow myself down, so I could respond and not react, was and is a difficult undertaking.

I was one and a half years clean and sober, popular in both Twelve Step programs, new to A Course in Miracles, driving a new Ford Ranger pickup, partners in a new business that I thought was doing well, and living on the beach (Siesta Beach), I was living the bachelors' dream but still alone and lonely.

There was still something gnawing away on my insides, a constant yearning for something more. I had no idea what, but I knew it was there. I would, as always, be led to what was next.

After a meeting one night my friend Deborah gave me a book *The Junkie Priest* and said, "Read this." Deborah had become someone I listened to and trusted. She said read it and I just followed her directions. The story was about Father Dan Egan. I would go down to the beach every night before the sunset and read this book. I was so deeply inspired by this man's story. He had walked out of his parish one evening to find a young lady standing in the cold. She looked sick and starving. She was a junkie. He knew nothing about that world but he was about to learn. He knew she needed help and he took her to the hospital. They wanted nothing to do with her or her kind. He was horrified that this young girl needed help and the hospital turned her away.

He made it his life's mission to help the addict. He lost his parish. I think he was made to leave his church but he didn't stop. They needed help and he committed himself to be the one to help them.

I would read every night and cry. I had never heard of anyone that was so giving of themselves. I wanted to be able to give so freely and not expect anything in return. My prayer changed. "God teach me what you would have me learn so I may do what you would have me do, and become what you would have me be. I am yours to do with as you will." I read the book and prayed that prayer every evening at sunset for over two weeks. Internally I was changing, again.

After two weeks of reading, crying and praying, one morning I went to work, to the business that I thought was doing so well, and asked my partner what was on the board for the day. He said, "Nothing, it's over." I shook my head and asked, rather quickly. "What's over?" He said, "The business, we have nothing, it's done."

I was in shock! 'What the hell had happened? How did I not know this?' I paused for a moment to reflect and it hit me! The prayer I had been praying to be taught, to be used ...

this was an answer to the prayer. I was at peace for a moment. I started to leave in the pickup. My partner said, "You can't take the truck." There went the peace. "What do you mean? I can't take the truck?" He said almost callously, "It is part of the business, it has to go back to the dealer."

In less than two weeks time, I lost the truck, the business, the apartment on the beach and I was living in a small bedroom that I couldn't even pay rent on. I just knew this was part of a bigger plan. I had moved into a friend's house using her spare bedroom. Now that I wasn't working I was going to at least two Twelve Step meetings a day and as many ACIM meetings as I could. Callie was having sessions with me pro bono and I was seeing her as often as her calendar would allow.

I was spending a lot of quiet time alone, just me and God. After about a week of living in my friend's bedroom I went for a walk one night and crying, I said to God, "I think I have bitten off more than I can chew. Maybe I don't want to be who you would have me be." After just a moment I returned, "No, if losing everything is part of becoming what you would want me to be, then bring it on."

The next day my friend told me I had to move out.

I was approaching thirty years old, one and a half years sober, dealing with the demons of my past and the ones from my childhood, trying to stay clean and sober, and I had nowhere to go.

I stayed with different friends in the fellowships for a while. I intuitively knew what I had to do. I needed to go back to Kentucky. There were fears I had to face and I needed to face them where they lived.

When I told Ed what I thought I needed to do, he totally disagreed. He said, "You are setting yourself up to drink and use again." It was the first time that I wasn't listening. It was really scary for me. I knew what I had to do, even if I didn't have Ed's support.

Callie supported me whole-heartedly. When I told her what I intended to do, she simply responded with a smile, "Go *learn* us some lessons." ACIM teaches "You are never healed alone."

There was another dragon to be faced ... and it was in Kentucky.

CHAPTER 10

THE MIRACLES

Once back in Kentucky, I took another detour before getting to His intended destination (the trailer). Along the way I found help with finding a job and finances for a car and the legal matters in front of me. An angelic person had been put in my path and was more than willing to play her part.

The job she helped me get was in a *treatment center.* Imagine that, me Johnnie Calloway, the boy that would never amount to anything working in a drug and alcohol treatment center! I felt like screaming to the heavens, "Yes I am Johnnie Calloway and I have amounted to something!"

My past was haunting me terribly now that I was back in Kentucky. The authorities had twenty-eight warrants out for my arrest due to the bad checks I had written nine years prior. The cloud of these and other wrongs weighed on me heavily. I could constantly hear Bill saying, "All the sooner you clean up your past the freer you will be to step into a new tomorrow."

I knew I had to clean these things up if I truly wanted to be what God intended for me to be. I had to put my new found faith to work.

I walked into the County courthouse one afternoon around four thirty. The first person I saw was the county sheriff.

Almost jubilantly he said, "Hey Johnnie, how ya been?" I answered, "Good, Sir, You?" He said, "Good, thanks. Man, it's been a long time. Where ya been?" My hasty response, "It's been nine years since I have been in this courthouse. I have been in Florida." To which he responded, "So why are you here now?" Reluctantly I told him, "You guys have some paperwork on me, I want to clear that up." With a smile, he said, "Good for you, young man. Let's see if I can help."

He called two of his deputies over, told them what he wanted and they went to the clerk's office. The sheriff and I chatted for a while about all the guys I used to get locked up with. Some of them were in jail as we spoke. It broke my heart to know they were still trapped in that lifestyle. Fifteen or twenty minutes went by and the two deputies came back. Once they reached the sheriff, they called him off to the side and started whispering. I fearfully thought, "Oh my God I have done something in a blackout that I don't remember."

He returned to me and said, "Johnnie it is too late in the day. The girls in the clerk's office have gone home for the day. My guys can't find your papers." I quickly stated, "That's okay I will just come back tomorrow." He said, "I know you will." I knew from his tone what he meant. I was going to jail. Before I could speak, he said, "Johnnie don't worry. I will come get you out myself first thing tomorrow morning, but it has been nine years since I last saw you. I don't want it to be another nine before I see you again."

A little over three years clean and sober, going to two different Twelve Step programs, with meetings every day, and I was going back to jail. I made peace with it though. Intuitively I knew it was truly the last time I would ever go to jail.

The next morning at seven o' clock sharp, the sheriff was there to get me. I had been one of the lucky ones in my earlier days with the police. They all liked me. I *never* gave them a hard time. Whenever they arrested me I just got in the car, with no resistance whatsoever.

I had watched my dad and sister be arrested many times as a child. They always resisted and still went to jail, only with bruises. Once, while being arrested, the officer (as I was getting in the backseat of the cruiser), jokingly said, "Johnnie boy, please don't take this wrong but I almost enjoy arresting you. Not that I like to see you go to jail but you never give me a hard time. You just get in the car." I laughed, "I don't need the bruises." I don't think he knew what I was referring to but he laughed with me.

The sheriff stuck to his word and got me out early. He did, however, give me a little lecture, "Johnnie you be sure and follow through with your intentions. You will be a better man for it and you will be able to walk with your head up." He then took me to get a court date. The date was set and I started praying, "God please help me to be honest with the judge and please help me to not abuse the name of the Twelve Steps to get myself out of trouble." I had known of several times in the fellowships where my friends had gone into court waving the Twelve Step flag (so to speak). I am not saying there is anything wrong with doing that but it wasn't what I wanted for myself. I wanted the truth to be enough.

My court date finally came. The Angel's financial assistance had helped me with the money to pay my fines on each check and the money for restitution on each check (a sizable amount). There were twenty eight checks. I had a pocketful of money that day.

As I sat before the judge (one that did not know me), he was rifling through all these papers. After a few minutes he looked up at me and asked, "Mr. Calloway, this was nineteen seventy

nine, it is now nineteen eighty eight, where have you been?"
Above all else I had prayed for the strength to be honest. I
responded, "It came time to come to court, I knew you all were
going to want money, I knew I didn't have any and I knew
you were going to want to lock me up. I knew I didn't want
to be locked up. I went to Florida." He actually laughed. Then
he asked, "Okay, so why are you back here now?" Without
even thinking I said, "I am tired of being paranoid and I want
this off my back." Again he laughed. I think the truth was
somewhat refreshing to him. He went back to going through
the many papers, looked up at me again and said, with a smile,
"Mr. Calloway most of these places are now out of business,
probably due to people like you."

He looked through the papers again. He looked at me
with a concerned look. He then said, "Mr. Calloway do you
have fifty dollars?" "Yes sir." I replied. Again with a smile,
"You take that money over to the clerk's office and you have
a good day."

God truly was on my side and the truth really was paying
off in huge dividends. Now I could almost go anywhere I
wanted in Kentucky without looking over my shoulder.

There were other amends that needed to be made. I had
to go to each of my sisters and make my apologies. I had
learned though, that truly making amends meant changing the
behavior. With my family and close friends I needed to become
the man they had always hoped for me to be anyway. In the
Twelve Steps we call it 'the living amends'.

One of the things I had done really ate at me. A friend's
younger brother was one of the many people to whom I had
sold *the truck*. He was actually the one that made payments on it
for a while. He had really trusted me. I hated that he had to be
a part of my feeding the beast. I searched him out, discovered

where he lived and went to his house. When he came to his door and saw who was there, he was shocked. "Man you've got a nerve!" was the way he answered the door. Meekly, "I know but I need to talk to you." He stepped back and allowed me in. I spoke of what I had done to him and verbally apologized. Before he could speak I said, "I am here to make it right." Skeptically he asked, "How do you intend to do that?" "I am here to give you your money back." His wife was now with us. I think they really needed that money at the time. "Good. Do you remember how much it was?" he asked. "Yes, I said, will you take a check?" He and his wife looked at each other immediately and in unison, smiled and knowing my history with checks asked, "Is it good?" I laughed with them, "Yes, I would not come here and go through this with you only to give you a bad check."

Then I took a few minutes to tell them that I was doing this as a part of my Twelve Step program and that I needed to do this kind of thing if I really wanted to stay clean and sober. The conversation ended with, "Thank you Johnnie, we really appreciate this and we are happy for you."

The detour had served its purpose. Now following His plan I could stand on solid ground and face the dragon on its own turf. Back to my dad's I went.

There I was, in the same single-wide trailer that I had grown up in, where all the insanity had occurred. I literally felt seven years old in a thirty year-old body. Everything provoked a memory. I thought I was going to go insane. Thank God for the Twelve Steps. I was still missing ACIM.

I had called Callie and asked what I could do about A Course in Miracles. She suggested I get the book *A Course in Miracles*. Callie directed me to The Foundation for Inner Peace. They handled/managed all dealings for ACIM. I told them my situation and that I was flat broke. They shipped me a book for five dollars. It was usually twenty five.

A Course in Miracles is a difficult read at best. I didn't really understand any of it. I would read for a while, get puzzled, and call Callie. She really was a tremendous help. Eventually she said I should start a class. I did not know how to do that but Callie reassured me that I could, so I did. I put an ad in the Paducah newspaper for anyone interested in ACIM classes.

I got a response to the ad from Barbara Miller who is still a close friend, twenty six years later. She and a few other ladies, Jean, Elizabeth, and Louise, had been meeting and studying A Course In Miracles for a while, but thought they could use some guidance. They were all quite a bit older than me. They invited me to their class and asked if I would lead it. It was absolutely amazing! As the leader of this class, I would read aloud with them and almost every paragraph prompted a question. The whole time I was silently praying, "God please help me to help them and help me to understand this book." I knew, based on my classes with Callie, that the answers we sought were in this book and I was determined to find them. In the class when the questions were asked, I would open my mouth to say, "I do not know what that means." Instead of that rolling off my tongue, I would say things that were answering their questions. The whole time I was rattling off the answers, part of my mind would be thinking "Wow! You had better be listening to this." I led that class and two others for my Twelve Step friends throughout the rest of my stay in Kentucky.

I was rebuilding my support team, which was a good thing because I was about to need it more than ever.

Living with my dad in that trailer was a *nightmare*. I was remembering everything; the beatings Jackie endured, the incest that she and I both endured, the incessant screaming, the pounding heartbeat, the need to be alert at all times. It was all there. The big difference was the physicality of it. I was thirty years old, not seven. I was two and a half inches taller than my dad, I outweighed him by twenty pounds and I was in much better shape than he was and ... he was fifty eight.

I could not keep myself conscious of the physical part. I was constantly feeling as though I was a little kid. It was very intense. I literally felt like I needed to jump up on the counter to reach the upper cabinets in the kitchen. In my heart and soul I was *seven*. The fear was just as intense as it had been when I was a kid. Just as before, I would count his steps when I went to bed, trying to anticipate which door he was going to open. I knew exactly how many steps it took for him to reach the first bedroom, how many for the bathroom and finally how many it took for the back room where I was staying.

One day I was home all day. I usually got myself out of there pretty early and stayed out until bedtime. This was a day for being home. Everything was a memory. I could *see* the blood on the wall from Jackie cutting her wrists, I could *hear* the pounding of his fist on someone's face or the sound of that thick black belt on someone's rear end. The nightmare of it all was consuming me and I was absolutely terrified.

Periodically I would remind myself of the physical differences. It wouldn't last long; I was trapped in that seven year-old mindset. He was drunk and just kept getting drunker as the day passed. He started arguing with my grandmother, cussing her and calling her every type of whore that he could think of. I was so caught up in being that little boy that I did nothing but listen.

When evening came I went as fast as I could to my meeting. I needed relief from the craziness and I needed to be around some sanity and to talk to someone that wasn't angry or afraid.

I came home from my meeting and the relief that it brought, only to be right back in the nightmare again. I thanked God for the break. I went down the hall (when I was a boy that hall always seemed to be a mile long, especially if I was listening for him) to the end bedroom and went to bed without speaking to him.

Soon after I went to bed he started meandering around the front of the house. "Is he angry? Is he looking for sex? Is he just hungry?" I was out of practice. I wasn't sure of his mood.

He started down the hall. I was counting every step. My heart was racing, I was sweating and I could feel my temples pulsing every time my heart beat. As he drew closer, I thought, "If he opens that door I am going to snap his fucking neck." Only to be followed with, "My God Johnnie, you are thinking about killing your dad." Then, "Yep, and I will be doing the world a favor."

He went to the bathroom. I silently cried my thirty-year-old/seven-year-old self to sleep.

The next day the memories were flooding my mind again and I could not escape them. Oddly, I was still aware that this was all part of God's plan but I could not imagine why He wanted me to be back in this mess or why He would want me to relive this hell.

The next night I was a nervous wreck. I didn't think I could endure one more moment. I knew that whatever God wanted me here for wasn't accomplished yet. I went for a walk and I talked with Him. "I really want to be and do what you want me to be and do, but I do not think I can do this. I am certain you want me here. But please let it come soon or I am going to snap." Periodically, I insanely thought He may have had me there so I could kill him.

After the walk, I went back to my grandmother's house (which was on the same property) and ate something. He was very drunk and very angry, screaming at my grandmother about who knows what, and then he went back to the trailer. Eventually, I had to go over to the trailer too.. He was sitting on the couch and as I walked past him, he was seething with anger.

I went to the back room and dressed for my meeting. When I got to the door to leave, he said in that gruff, gravelly voice of his, "Boy, where in the hell are you going?" I responded with the voice of the seven-year-old, almost shyly, "I'm going to my meeting."

He jumped off the couch like a cat going after a mouse, "I think I will just whip your ass." I finally snapped. I walked over to him, put my nose one inch from his and I screamed, "Go ahead put a hand on me. Give me permission to snap your fucking neck." He turned sheet white, went back to the couch, sat down, and said, "I can't do that anymore, I am too old." I wouldn't have thought it possible but my rage went to a whole other level. I screamed, "Oh but when you were a young man and my sister was a little girl, you beating the hell out of her made all the sense in the world. When you were a young man and my grandmother was an old lady, you beating the hell out of her made all the sense in the world. And ... when you were a young man and my frail, tiny grandfather pissed you off about anything, you beating the hell out of him made all the sense in the world. Now I am the young man and you are the old man and now you want to get fucking logical." All the while I was right in his face screaming. It sobered him. A huge alligator tear started to roll down his cheek. Believe it or not my rage escalated. I screamed again, "Don't you even pretend to care now." I think for the first time ever I was about to hit him. A voice spoke in my head and said, "You will never forgive yourself if you do this." Calmly, I said, "Something just saved you." Then I walked out the door.

Prior to that interaction, my father never respected anything I had to say. He would literally ask me a question and turn and walk away as I would be trying to answer. After that interaction he hung on my every word. It was weird. I didn't understand. I shared the story once with one of the older gentlemen at a meeting and he told me, "That's simple Johnnie, in that one moment you accomplished two things: One, you demanded his respect and two, you broke through his denial."

Afterward I found myself letting go of the flood of memories that consumed me in the trailer. I found myself being able to sit and watch television with him as I had as a child. The confusing thing about my childhood was I *always* loved my dad, even when I hated him.

My dad had a gentle side, a very gentle side. He was such a Dr. Jekyl and Mr. Hyde. When I was younger I loved to watch television with him when he wasn't drinking. We made a game of it. When an actor would make their first appearance on a show, we raced to identify them and the last show we had seen them in.

Between the ages of nine and thirteen we only had three television stations, ABC, NBC and CBS. Late at night there would be the late movie, the late, late movie and the late, late, late movie. Sometimes, when sober, he would get me out of bed and say, "C'mon boy, our boys are on." That meant Jimmy Cagney, Humphrey Bogart, John Wayne or some other *hero* was on. He would then take me to the living room with him, pull me next to him and hold me close with his arm around me. I remember the incredible sense of safety I felt. I could breathe and the world was a good place to be. Then I would fall asleep, a *real* sleep.

One evening after the interaction where I almost hit him, we were watching a show about child abuse. He was on one end of the couch and I was on the other. I was curious as to how this show was affecting him. He told me. He started talking about his childhood. He had never done anything even remotely like that before. I was having a real conversation with my father. He became real for me in that moment. I already knew some of his history from previous stories from other people, but never had I gotten any of it from him.

He told me, "My dad kicked me and Momma out of the house when I was just three. Momma had nowhere to go and we ended up in Detroit. One day when I was eleven and skipping school, this guy and three boys showed up knocking at the door. I went to the door and the man asked for me by name. I told him, I was Alvie Calloway."

Then the man responded with, "Hello, my name is also Alvie Calloway. I am your father and these are your brothers." My dad told him he was *full of it*, and that his *dad* was at work. My dad said to me in a very sincere and gentle voice, "Johnnie I grew up thinking Earl Page was my dad. I loved him. This guy shows up, tells me *he's* my dad and ruins my already ruined life. From that day forward I hated Earl Page. I didn't see my real dad again until I was almost twenty one. He came into my life just long enough to take Earl from me and then he was gone again."

Earlier in Florida, I had shared in a meeting one day that I really wanted and needed to forgive my dad. After the meeting this elderly gentleman cornered me and asked, "Do you really want to forgive your dad?" I responded, "They say my resentments will eat me alive and cause me to drink again if I don't." The older gentleman said in a soft and kind way,

"Then you need to take a look into his childhood instead of staying stuck in your own."

After my dad told me his story about his dad and his step dad, I decided I would look further into his childhood. I didn't have to look far. I asked his buddy Jiggs, who had known him from childhood. Jiggs, what was Daddy's childhood like?" Softness and a sense of true caring came over him when he told me about my dad. "Are you sure you want to know?" "Absolutely." I said. Jiggs told me, "Your dad was molested a lot as a kid, I believe by both men and women." My first thought, 'No wonder he is so sexually messed up.'

There were other stories ... my dad had come home from school one day (when he was fifteen) and his step dad was beating the hell out of my grandmother. My dad lost it and stabbed his step dad fifteen times, didn't kill him, but ended up in the Air Force for his efforts.

I was now starting to have a sense of true empathy for my dad. He was indeed human. After he opened up and told me about his real father, we started to have a relationship. I was falling in love with the ogre in my life.

I was still going to ACIM classes and Twelve Step meetings as often as I could. Even though all these miracles were going on he was still drinking and having his moments. And when he did, I was still seven and afraid, but it wasn't the same. I wasn't quite as afraid and I didn't feel quite as alone. Something inside me had shifted.

The strange thing that I never understood, with all the abuse and all the craziness I had lived in, was that it was the little things that I resented the most. For instance, he never told me he loved me unless he was drunk, he never said he was proud of me and he never acknowledged the wrongs he had done. Those things seem small compared to all the other abuses, but those are the ones that I held onto.

I was sitting up late one night after he had gone to bed, studying ACIM for my class for the next night. He had gone to bed sober after we watched a television program. He woke up and shouted into the living room, "Boy what the hell are you doing in there this late?" I said, "Studying for my class for tomorrow night." He knew it was a class I was teaching. Next thing I know he is standing in front of me in his underwear. "Johnnie I don't think I have ever bothered to tell you how proud I am of how you've turned your life around. I am proud of you son." One of those seldom seen tears started to roll out of his eye and down his cheek. "I really don't think I have ever said I love you unless I was drunk. I do love you son." He turned and started back to bed. As he got to the hall entrance he turned and he said, "And I apologize for not being the father you deserved."

I was speechless. I was seriously choked up. Awestruck could be a way of saying how I felt. Everything I had ever wanted from him had just been given me in a two minute period. The things he said were more than just orchestrated words. They seriously came from his heart. There was no thought behind them, no plan, he just poured them out and they were real! My dad had never been one to show his emotions. Even *he* couldn't hold back the emotion he felt in that moment.

And in that moment everything he had ever done was alright. And I knew why God had wanted me back in Kentucky.

I was reading *A Course in Miracles* when he came into the room that evening. After my dad, the dragon in my life, walked back out of that room, he had given me the best gift that I had ever been given. He gave me a dad, even if it was for only a moment. But it wasn't. From that day forward my dad and I were friends. We never cussed each other again, not even if he was drunk. A true miracle had transpired.

There were several miracles that occurred for us after that. Listening to a country song one afternoon I let go of some of my self-centeredness around my dad. Through the words of a country song, "Keep it Between the Lines" by Ricky Van Shelton I realized that after a lifetime of me being upset over not *having* a dad, he didn't get to *be* a dad.

Through A Course in Miracles I was learning about forgiveness and the importance of it. With my dad, I had just forgiven the biggest violator of my life. I guess I thought I was done. I certainly was not. There were still dragons in the closet yet to be dealt with.

I still had work to do in Kentucky. I was still teaching the ACIM class, I had a sponsor to consult with and those I sponsored to attend to, but I knew my time back in Kentucky was almost over. Closure was something that was foreign to me. I usually just left when I was done. The Twelve Step fellowships and the ACIM classes had taught me about responsibility in relationships. I needed to say my goodbyes and let the people who loved me know I appreciated all they had done for me. There were many that had played major roles in the miracles that were now my life. I had a debt to pay to them and for most of them it simply meant to be the man they had helped me to become and to pass on what had been passed on.

I had faced the dragon I had come to Kentucky for. I did not conquer him, but *that* one had been tamed.

CHAPTER 11

THE RESPITE

Almost four years had passed since I started my new life. I had been chasing my recovery like I was in a race with someone. In the earlier part of my recovery I had been told by many, "If you put fifty percent of the energy into your recovery that you put into your addictions, you will be fine." I had really tried to put in an equal amount. I hadn't but I did try.

After Kentucky I came back to Florida. I was emotionally tired. My heart had been through the proverbial mill. Now was a time for just living; being what I had learned or as best I could anyway. Living the principles of the Twelve Steps and ACIM is not easy. No one does it perfectly. Operating within the parameters of what I had learned was now my main objective.

In the four years I had studied diligently the philosophies of the programs, I had done everything in my power to become 'that guy'; the one the new guys could follow. I had acquired the respect of my peers. To some degree I had come to have self respect.

Now I just wanted to be done. There was still more work to do but I was tired.

I was over four years clean and sober and still going to a Twelve Step meeting every day. I no longer went because I felt like I would drink or drug if I didn't. I went because I loved them. I loved/love the people in them. I love what we do before and after the meetings. The camaraderie is enjoyable. Those people were now my extended family and going to a meeting every night was the equivalent of going home after work for dinner with the family.

I was now learning to have fun. I had always had plenty of laughs in my recovery. My before life had provided me with plenty of comedic material. My time in recovery had certainly provided me with it as well.

I found a place to live. I went back to work in air conditioning (my main source of income since my first arrival in Florida) and became as close as possible to being "normal." Normal and Johnnie have been quite an oxymoron.

I was just living life. When I am focused on my work I usually make decent money. My ego won't let me do anything half way at least if it is something I want to be doing. I became very good with air conditioning installation. Like everything else I wanted to stand out and to be the best.

In the four years of chasing my spiritual growth I had acquired an insatiable appetite for learning. I wanted/needed to know more; more about the human condition, more about how the heart and mind could work in unison and more than anything else I wanted to know and acquire an even better understanding of the God of *my* understanding.

The appetite started to gnaw at me again. Sue, Ed's wife, went to see a psychic astrologer, Mary Padlak. Sue was absolutely blown away by what she learned from Mary through having her "chart" read. Sue shared with me everything that Mary had shared with her. I thought it was all malarkey. I intended to prove to Sue that to believe in that crap was insane.

Sue, Ed, and I, along with a few other friends, planned a trip to a Twelve Step retreat in Lantana Florida. Mary Padlak lived and worked out of Boca Raton Florida. I thought the best way to help Sue was to see the lady myself and then I could let Sue in on the scam. I therefore scheduled an appointment with Mary while I was on the East Coast for the retreat.

I was with Mary for a little over three hours, with my jaw on the floor. I was astonished. The entire time I was with Mary I was avidly looking for the proof she was a hoax. She told me about thoughts I had that no one else knew. She did.

Listening very intently for the evidence, she said, "Your mother died from something sexual." That was it! This was the one place she was wrong. My mother died from cancer. I told Mary this and she responded, "Yes, cancer of the uterus. Right?" The wind was let out of my sails. This lady was for real. She then said, "That makes perfect sense. Cancer is a disease of repression and wherever we hold our guilt is where it will show up. Your mother felt ashamed about being raped by her father and that is where she repressed it."

How in the hell did she know my granddad had raped my mom? It was scary.

She told me about the abuse of my childhood. She then opened a door to my belief system. Ed had nudged me in the direction of questioning my entire belief system about God, which had led to questioning my entire belief system about everything. She said, "You came here to learn about the receiving side of abuse. In another life you yourself were an abuser. And you did a good job of choosing your teacher."

'Oh my God! This lady was talking about past lives! Okay so she is a nut.' But ... I could not deny that it just felt right.

She went on to tell me about money in my life. "Money is never going to happen for you Johnnie, until you write."

In utter disbelief I asked, "Write? Write what?" She quickly volleyed, "Don't play dumb with me. You know what you need to write about but it scares you because you don't remember learning it." I quickly put it together, she is now implying that I have learned things in one of these past lives that I need to write about.

She had just made a turn that I wasn't sure I could follow her on. The door to my open mind was only so big and she was trying to drive a semi truck through it. But ... it felt right. If this is so it could answer so many more of the questions I still had.

She had opened my mind to many new ideas. Fortunately I had a weekend planned for the retreat and plenty of time to think.

I thought about the possibility of past lives and choosing your own parents and what that all could mean. More importantly I thought, 'Even if it *is* so, how does that help me in today's world?' Eventually I just let it go. Or so I thought.

I spent the weekend at the retreat talking to Ed and getting his opinion on all of it. He didn't have a lot to say to me about past lives or ACIM. I spoke with anyone actually that would talk on such matters. Some were totally open and others not at all.

About two weeks after I was home from the retreat, I got a call one afternoon from Mary Padlak. As soon as she said her name I thought, "I paid her. What the hell could she want?" We went through the pleasantries, then she asked, "Are you writing?" I was very confused, "No." She then said the strangest thing, "Part of my job now is to make sure you write." My thought, 'Okay it is official, she is over the top.'

After that she called me at least once a week with the same routine. I started having anger issues coming up. I was experiencing anger like I had never experienced anger before. I was getting angry with store clerks over nothing, little old ladies in checkout lanes ... everyone was a potential target for my ire.

I was installing duct work on a twelve story condo during the time. One day the foreman confronted me in front of several other tradesmen. I became enraged, started walking toward him, taking my tool belt off and visualized throwing him off the fourth floor. Just as I reached him that Voice butted in, "He's not even who you are angry with." Just like with my dad, the voice had saved us both. I turned and walked away.

Mary called again, this time was different though. I had gotten used to her calls and now I actually looked forward to them. This call, her first words were, "You've been experiencing a lot of anger haven't you?" I had to ask, "How the hell did you know?" She chuckled, "I just know you." She didn't know me, she spent three hours with me when she read my chart and that was it.

She continued, "I am having an anger intensive workshop this weekend. You are supposed to be there." Quickly I said, "I can't afford that." She responded, "All you have to do is get here. You can stay at my retreat and I won't charge you for the workshop. You really need to do this or you will never write." "Okay, okay already. I will be there."

My recovery took me on many adventures. I never zip lined, climbed mountains, went scuba diving or sailed the seven seas but the emotional adventures I traveled were incredible. Here I go off to participate in an "Anger Intensive Weekend" and I was about to have an experience like no other. It was going to open a whole new way of healing for me to go even deeper than I thought was possible.

Re-enactments

I didn't know anyone in this workshop but Mary. There were about eight of us at Mary's place for the workshop. Everyone was really nice. It reminded me of a Twelve Step meeting or an ACIM class in as much as the diversity of the people there. There was a doctor, an electrician, a waitress, a stay-at-home mom and I was the resident AC guy. I do not remember everyone but I will never forget the things that happened.

A 're-enactment' consists of someone taking an experience or collection of experiences from their life that had an impact on them (usually a negative impact) and re-enacting it. You lay out the scene and ask others to play roles for you so you can relive the scene. After they help you relive it, they then help you create a 'do-over'.

The first one was very intense for me to watch. A very small lady (I do not remember her name) was reliving a scene with her mom. She got so angry in the re-enactment that she actually threw an ashtray at the woman playing her mom.

I was thirty-two years old, a little over five years clean and sober, and still very active and strong. I knew that if I got that angry someone might get hurt. Therefore I just backed up and leaned against the wall.

Mary knew what was going on with everyone in that room at any given moment throughout the entire weekend. She knew immediately that I had checked out. When she could free herself from the activity she came and leaned beside me asking, "Where did you go?" I responded, "Mary I do not want to make it sound like I am some kind of badass or something but if you get me that angry, you don't have anyone in here that can contain me." To which she responded, "Would you please just trust me and the process?" I quietly said, "I guess."

Next it was my turn. Mary put me in a corner of the room and totally covered me in pillows. The only thing you could see was my head and shoulders. One guy had the role of my dad. He was a big black guy with a deep voice. I instructed him on how to be my dad, with the bigger than life gravelly voice, the stern matter of fact demeanor and the physical prowess.

The younger lady played Jackie's part. She was small but had a strong presence, almost cocky. This girl fit the part of Jackie. My mom was covered up in a sheet playing dead. And my grandmother was played by a sassy older lady. Those were the main characters in my life as a child.

The scene: My dad was standing over me continually raising his hand to slap me, screaming that he had it with me and I was going to get it. Jackie was constantly stepping between us to protect me, and my grandmother was repeatedly saying, "He's just lying, he's always lying." My mom would raise up and uncover herself to say, "I can't help you now son, you have to do this yourself."

Mary instructed me to tell them to stop. They were all screaming. Everything was really loud. Mary had to tell me a few times to tell them to stop. Finally I said like a mouse, "Stop." Everyone just kept screaming. Mary said, "Listen to them. Do you really think that this bunch heard you?" I said again just a little louder than the first time, "Stop." Mary laughed, "If you want this group to stop, you are going to have to mean it." The lady playing my mom said over and over, "I can't help you son."

I eventually screamed over and over and over, "Stop!!!" They all settled down. I thought, 'man I am glad that is over,' and I started to get up. Mary was not through. She directed the gentleman playing my dad to take one of the pillows and hold it. That pillow represented my power and my dad had control of *all* my power. "Johnnie," she said, "these people hold all of your power. You have never gotten to be who you are. You have always been who you think these people want you to be. Are you ready to be yourself and who you would like to be?" Meekly again I responded, "Yes, I think so."

"You *think* so? No Johnnie you are going to have to mean it. In order for you to take your power back you are going to have to be committed to taking it. They have had it for a very long time and they do not want to give it up."

The one holding my pillow at the time was the doctor. I thought, 'This will be easy enough, I will just take it from him.' Mary read me like a book. Before I got to the standing position she had *all* of them get a grip on that pillow. I pulled and tugged and fought to get my pillow. I couldn't do it. Mary, then said, "You have got to mean it, tell them you are the owner of your power and when you say it, *mean* it."

By now I was screaming as loud as I possibly could, constantly pulling and nothing was giving. Mary was all over the place telling the people what to say and to not let go. I was seriously giving it all I had. I wanted control of my life and they had it.

"You can't do this by yourself. You need to ask for help." I was determined I could do this without anyone's help. I kept screaming and pulling, all to no avail. Eventually I squeaked out, "Someone help." Mary asked, "Do you mean it? Do you really want help? Or do you still think you can do this by yourself?" With some conviction I said, "I really need help. I want my life back." Mary asked, "Back? Do you think you ever had your life? Ask them again for help." I asked, "Please help."

Mary had the rest of the group stand up and get on my side of the pillow and help me take my pillow/power. When the scene was over almost the whole group was in tears. The rest of the weekend I carried that pillow with me. Mary even asked if I would like to take it back to Sarasota with me.

I re-enacted two more scenes. I felt like the entire weekend was for me. I left to go back to Sarasota on Sunday but it was Thursday before I had a voice and could tell my friends what had happened.

After I got back to Sarasota, Mary continued to call to see how I was. She was still asking if I was writing. Mary held group therapy sessions in her house once a week and was pretty determined that I needed them. She was, to say the least, committed and relentless. She never gave up on me.

Finally, I think to get her to leave me alone, I moved to Del Ray Beach. I moved into Mary's retreat.

In my quest, I had learned about 'cellular memory' … how we store the energy of events in our lives in our bodies. These memories can control us. Mine did and they needed to be released, or else I would never write and now I knew … *I was going to write!*

CHAPTER 12

THE BOOK

I was almost six years clean and sober, thirty-three years old, still going to Twelve Step meetings every day, teaching/facilitating A Course in Miracles classes in Del Rey Beach Florida, while also living at my therapist's retreat and avidly seeking new methods to learn and heal.

Living with your therapist can be tricky. It was worth it. She got to see what I was like in the world. Mary helped me learn to let go of the past. I had done a lot of the work on forgiving my dad and my family. Mary opened the door for me to forgive myself.

I still was not writing. Mary wasn't pushing it anymore, not for the writing anyway. She was and is one of the wisest people I know. She just has a way about her that made me feel comfortable with growing outside the box.

I was starting to really open to new ideas. In therapy I was being taught about cellular memory, what may trigger it and how it can be released. I was introduced to Stevie. Stevie taught me about rebirthing. 'Rebirthing' is a healing technique that uses the breath to access and release cellular memory.

I was in therapy sessions with Mary once a week and having two or three rebirthings a week. The blocks that had held me back my entire life were being removed rapidly.

Mary had a male counterpart in our group therapy sessions, Michael. Michael was great. In the healing fields, in therapy, the Twelve Steps, ACIM classes and workshops there is a statement that is heard frequently, 'You are only as sick as your secrets.' I have always taken issue with the statement. One night in our group Michael said to one of the clients, "You are only as sick as your secrets." I laughed. Michael looked at me and asked, "What is so funny?" I replied, "That is absolute shit." Michael asked, "Why would you say that?" I answered, "Because it isn't true. I have no secrets and I am still sick as hell." Michael looked like I had thrown cold water in his face, and asked, "What do you mean you have no secrets?" I said, "I have no secrets. There is nothing that I have ever done that I haven't shared at this point with someone."

Michael was stunned. He looked puzzled and then it was like a light went on for him. "Johnnie, I know what you do. You tell everyone all the filth on yourself and you never let anyone know who you want to be or what your dreams are. The new you is your secret. What are your dreams and aspirations?"

What my dreams and aspirations were weren't anyone's business. He pressed on, "What are your dreams Johnnie?" I was almost whispering when I said, "I want to be an author." He looked more puzzled now than ever. He paused, shook his head and said, "This is going to sound absolutely insane but please trust me here. If you shave the beard and cut that hair of yours and let go of that dumb country boy image of yours, you *will* write." He went on to say, "Between now and next session you need to write something to read to the group."

I had a full beard and hair to the bottom of my shoulder blades. After group that night I shaved the beard. That beard had been with me for over sixteen years. It was a part of my identity. That night I wrote "The Boy and the Monster," which eventually became "The Boy and the Dragon" (the third chapter of my first book to come, *Taming the Dragon*).

Before group the following week, I had cut my hair. I believed in following the directions of those I was paying to give me direction. It seemed to make sense to me. In group, Michael had me read the story. I was terrified. I had only written my poems at that time, never had I written a story. And only my closest friends ever got to hear those poems. Now the whole group was going to hear the story I had written.

While reading I never looked up, I just stared at the paper. When I was finished it took me several minutes to look at the group. When I did look up they were all either smiling or crying.

Upon getting that response from the group for reading "The Boy and the Monster", I could not stop writing. I became obsessed with writing and I became determined for my writings to become a book.

In my Twelve Step meetings and my ACIM classes I became 'the guy that is writing the book.' My head swelled. Everyone was asking about the book. In my mind I was now "that guy"; the one the newcomers could and would follow. I had arrived.

Totally overlooking that my life was a mess, I was totally absorbed in the writing and not taking care of business. I had moved from Mary's into a halfway house (a home for newcomers in the Twelve Steps while making the transition). I was over six years sober. Of course in my mind this was okay (I was writing the book).

There was a couple, Ron and Sue, who were helping me immensely with the writing and editing. Someone led me to my publisher. He said that he had also been involved in the early stages of the printing of *A Course in Miracles*. He initially reported to me that he had published ACIM. For me this was just too perfect ... Divine order at work!

Several of my recovering friends suggested, "Slow down."

The book was finished, published and I had over one hundred copies. The kid who would never amount to anything was an author! They sold very rapidly but the response was not as I had anticipated. The editing was very poorly done. They had told me they were good and I just went on trust. It is very difficult for me to proof-read my own writing. As I re-read I saw what I *meant* to be there, not necessarily what *was* there. The stories in *Taming the Dragon* were deep and meaningful. They were stories, a metaphor of my life. They had been poorly put together. I did have a message but that did not make me the "second coming."

In the book *Twelve Steps and Twelve Traditions* it clearly states, "It was only by repeated humiliations that we were forced to learn something of humility. It was only at the end of a long road, marked by successive defeats and humiliations, and the final crushing of our self sufficiency, that we began to feel humility as something more than a condition of groveling despair." I wasn't even close. I was no longer facilitating A Course in Miracles classes, but I thought, 'I *am* the teacher! As I should be. After all, look at what all I had accomplished! Look at how devoted I had been to my recovery. I knew! And you should listen!'

The book did not bring me the instant success that I had anticipated. It brought me a lot of disappointment and heartache.

Just before the book was completed, I met '*her*'. Louise. She was the one … she was the payoff for all my hard work. She would be what would make it all worthwhile. She was such a breath of fresh air for me. She made everything fun. Fun had become quite a foreign concept. I still laughed a lot but I did not do anything fun. Everything had been about the book. With Louise I got to play … something I had forgotten.

Unfortunately my time with Louise was short-lived. When Louise and I started hanging out together, there had been a boyfriend. When we met he was in Miami helping them recover from Hurricane Andrew. She told me he had been verbally and emotionally abusive to her.

I moved in with Louise and just a few days later, my mom's mom (Momma Trixie) passed away. Louise bought me a round trip ticket home. I wasn't back in Del Ray twenty four hours before I got the call saying my dad's step-dad (Poppa) had passed. I was a wreck.

Fortunately, I had been given an additional round trip ticket on the trip for my grandmother's funeral, because the airline messed up the scheduling and I had to lay over in St. Louis. Louise told me that the boyfriend was coming back from Miami. It just so happened that it was the same day I was leaving for the second funeral. She promised she would tell him it was over, and that she had met me. The plan was for me to call her later that night after all had settled down with my family back in Kentucky.

I had taken copies of my manuscript with me on the trip for my grandmother's funeral. I had given one to my dad.

Later that night I had called Louise several times and gotten no answer. My stomach was in that old familiar knot. I knew! I finally called Louise's roommate, Lori. I asked Lori where Louise was and she almost whispered, "Johnnie, I do not want to be in the middle of this." to which I replied, "Lori, darlin', you already are."

Louise came to the phone. I immediately asked, "Louise, where is he?" She answered, "He is in bed." I asked, "What bed?" She said, "Mine." My heart broke. I had lost a grandmother and a grandfather in a very short time and now I was losing her also. I was devastated.

When I got off the phone with Louise my dad was sitting across the room from me (sober). When I started to cry, in a voice with a gentleness that I had never heard him use, he said, "Son you may want to remember what you have written." *'He read it!* He actually read my book!' The healing that occurred for me in that moment was more powerful than any rebirthing or re-enactment that I had ever endured. It was a gift that I let myself fully receive.

With Louise, I felt like I had done all the work for nothing. This was not supposed to be happening. I was supposed to end up with the girl. She was to be my prize for all the effort that I had put in to my recovery.

After my grandfather's funeral I was quick to go back to Del Rey and face the music. I was trying with all my heart to practice the spiritual principles that I had learned in my travels.

When I got to Louise's to get my things, I said to her, "You obviously still need to learn what you can from someone who will verbally and emotionally abuse you. I cannot be that teacher for you. You can go be with him and I hope I will be around when you are through."

Walking away from her, leaving her with him, was one of the most difficult things I had ever done. I had to find a place, quick and I did. I always do.

Even though the book was finished, the windfall of money did not come with it. I had been very naïve about the literary world.

I rented a room from a friend (I rented the master bedroom because he needed the extra money) and I got a job in Air Conditioning again and decided I didn't need to be the one to save the planet. Still in my heart, *'I wrote the book!'*

I went to a workshop on ACIM where they only asked for a love offering. After the workshop I met the key speaker and gave him a copy of *Taming the Dragon*, as my 'Love Offering'. We chatted a bit and he told me about his retreat in the Ozark Mountains.

I had only been renting the room for a couple of weeks when my roommate came in and said, "I have some really good news." I liked him so I excitedly asked, "So what's up?" He happily responded, "My girlfriend's moving in." I said, "That is really cool, I am happy for you." Then he said, "Since it will be two of us, we will need the master bedroom." I said, "Okay, I don't need all that room anyway." But then he said, "Well, she needs the second room for storage." This was on a Tuesday. My heart sank and I said, "When is this taking place?" "Friday", was his response. I came back with, "Oh so your good news for me is I've got until Friday to move?" He said, "Yeah, sorry." And that was that.

I immediately went outside and asked God, "What do I do now?" The name of the speaker with the retreat in the Ozarks came to my mind. Out of curiosity I called him and told him my predicament. He asked if I was handy with tools. I told him I could do about anything. We made an agreement. He would help me promote my book if I would, in turn, maintain his retreat, but I had to commit to six months.

So I was off to another spiritual adventure.

CHAPTER 13

THE FALL

I left Del Rey for The Ozark Mountains and a retreat named 'The Center'. First I stopped in Sarasota for a visit with my old friends and hopefully to sell some books. I had almost no money. I was driving a Buick Electra 225. I do not remember what model year the car was but it was a boat. It was old and not the most reliable car in the world.

The morning I left Sarasota, I stopped at the metaphysical bookstore in the Unity Church and bought a copy of *The Miracle* by Og Mandino and I took off. I had read one of his earlier books, *The Choice* and I loved it. It had done for me what Richard Bach's book *Illusions* had done for me, which was to fill my heart with hope and inspiration.

All my goodbyes were said and my friends had expressed their concerns about what I was doing, where I was headed, and what I was driving. Being my adventurous self, I didn't listen. I had faith that whatever I got myself into, God would get me out of. He always did, even before I quit drinking and drugging.

Just north of Tampa that car overheated. I pulled over to look for water and didn't have any luck. So I decided that I should sit on the guard rail and read my new book. I had been there for a little while when some county trucks pulled up in the median right in front of me. I ran over and told them my situation. A couple of them laughed and got a five gallon water can out of their truck and helped me fill up the radiator.

I was no more than five minutes down the road and it was overheating again. I took the first exit and was starting to have doubts about my trip. There were a couple of service stations right off the exit. I pulled into a Shell station, told them what was going on with the Buick and they quoted me a price of three hundred sixty dollars. I only had one hundred and twenty dollars and still had a long way to go in this car that was using up gas like crazy. The attendant told me there was a radiator shop across the street.

I pulled into the shop and told the gentleman my predicament. He did not give me time for the rest of the story and quickly said, "I have that radiator in my other shop just down the street." and jumped in his truck and took off.

There was a Burger King in the adjoining parking lot, so I thought, 'I had better eat before he gets all my money.' Before I was through with my burger he drove up with the radiator. I finished eating and went back to the shop. Then I told him the rest of the story. "I only have one hundred and ten dollars, I have to get all the way to a spiritual retreat in the Ozark Mountains to do volunteer work and this car I'm driving is a gas guzzler." He studied for a moment then asked, "Do you have anything of value in the car?" I had already noticed the state that his truck was in … a faded red pickup that was terribly oxidized. It just so happened that as a way of making some money, I had been selling car wax out of my trunk. I still had a few cases of it with me. I knew I could make his truck look beautiful again. "Can I show you something?" "Sure", he said.

I took a very small amount of the wax and did a spot right in front of his windshield. He was amazed. He then responded,

"I have got to make a little money to cover my expense on the radiator. How about you wax my truck while I do your radiator, you give me forty dollars and two bottles of the wax and we will call it even?" I was ecstatic, "Absolutely." And that is what we did. I was back on the road in about one and a half hours and I still had seventy bucks.

My next stop was Kentucky, to visit with family, work in tobacco for a couple of days and recoup some of my funds before going on to The Ozarks.

My expectations of The Center were far different than what I found when I arrived. No one had actually told me what to expect, but I had certain pictures in my mind. I had imagined that there would be a community, with several people working the place, that the workshops/intensives would be constant, and that I would be surrounded by like-minded people all the time.

Instead, the leader (the owner of The Center) his wife and their two kids, an older gentleman named Glen and I made up The Center. I was disappointed to say the least. I wanted community. I spoke with the leader himself about how I felt and he told me there was an intensive coming up and to be patient. I was.

I was told upon arrival, "no caffeine, no nicotine and we eat live food." I was fine with no caffeine, and I had never smoked a cigarette in my life so I was fine with that but ... live food? I was curious, 'What the hell is live food?' For our first meal that evening bean sprouts and raw potatoes were put on the table.

Inside I screamed, 'Hell no! I really want to make this work but bean sprouts with no dressing even? And a raw potato? Okay so there has to be something else.' I ate with them as best I could. Eventually I gravitated to watermelon and almonds. For the four and a half months I was at The Center I predominantly ate watermelon and almonds. Once or twice a week I would sneak into town for my traditional biscuits and gravy.

There were no Twelve Step meetings within fifty miles of where I was in Missouri. There were no ACIM classes and the leader of The Center was gone to do workshops a lot. I was working forty to fifty hours every week. It was on a voluntary basis although I was paid one hundred dollars a month plus room and board.

Once a month I would drive over to Kentucky for a day or two to work in tobacco to be able to pay my car insurance and have gas money. I also needed a break from time to time. The workshops were infrequent at best. I think there were two a year plus 'work week' which was a week provided for past participants of workshops to come and volunteer their services, share the beauty of The Center and do healing classes, rebirthing, re-enactments, ACIM classes and other healing activities.

I absolutely loved the Ozark Mountains. I believe it is one of the most beautiful places in the world and the people there are really friendly. Two of the most spiritual experiences of my life were canoeing the rivers in the Ozarks.

When the workshops weren't going on, and it was mostly Glen and I on the property, I got terribly lonely and bored. In Theodosia there was a little bar and restaurant with a pool table. I would go up at night and play pool. I was always a pretty good pool player. I only drank soda and told all the guys I played with that I was an alcoholic and a drug addict and therefore did not want to party with them. They were all very respectful of my situation. I do not remember one time that any of them tried to sway me in their direction. I always appreciated them for that.

My trips to Kentucky became more frequent. I was really enjoying working in the tobacco fields again. My old friends (my old drinking buddies), who I worked with there, always had a way of glorifying the insanity of my youth, and loved telling stories of my wild adventures. The fact that I wasn't going to any Twelve Step meetings, or ACIM classes, that I was feeling lonely and hadn't had a girlfriend in a long time, were all the ingredients needed for a disaster.

For over six and a half years, until this point, I had been feeding the beast, by attending meetings, classes, book-writing, rebirthing, re-enactments and whatever positive activities I could offer it. These were all keeping me on track and helping me heal. But in the absence of these, the beast had acquired a new appetite and that appetite and was getting ferocious.

Now on the trips to Kentucky, rather than do what I knew I needed, I would just hang out with a relative, and be her live-in designated driver.

I felt as though everything in my safe little world was turned upside down, and that God had abandoned me. I was angry. Nothing that had nurtured me and made me whole was present in my life anymore.

Eventually even *I* realized I was in trouble. There were a few people at The Center at the time and in our class I told on myself and reported "I need a Twelve Step meeting." One of the classmates (not an alcoholic) responded, "Don't you think that is a crutch you've used long enough." That was all I needed ... support in not finding a meeting.

Also as a result of *the book* and me thinking I had become "that guy", I had become filled with what I now call "Twelve Step pride and spiritual arrogance" and could not bring myself to walk into a meeting and ask for help. Pride will absolutely kill a drug addict or alcoholic and mine had me by the throat. In my mind, 'I wrote the book; everyone would think it was all a lie.' And I asked myself, 'Was it?' I was in hell again and a paralyzing loneliness was upon me.

On one of the trips to the tobacco fields ... *she* was there; a girl I had been absolutely obsessed with in high school when I was in the tenth grade, a year before I was sent to the Boy's Camp. The bad thing then, was she was too young. She was beautiful and had a body that well exceeded her years. She looked like Daisy Duke from *The Dukes of Hazard*. At that time I had avoided her, but now, in the tobacco field I was thirty three and she was twenty eight ... not too bad, except she was married, and she was still beautiful.

Jill had a mean streak and I knew it. Usually when I was in a tobacco field I was in the lead with the other good workers. This day I was behind everyone so she and I could talk. She asked if I would come to her house for lunch. I laughed and said, "Hell no, I am not going to be alone with you anywhere." She smiled and sheepishly asked, "Why not?" I shook my head, "No way!"

In our conversation I had told her that my friend was in the hospital and I had to go there after work to visit. When I walked into the hospital room, my friend's mom said, "Here is Jill's phone number" and handed me the note. I looked at the number, held it in front of her and said in total seriousness, "This is trouble." She said, "Then don't call her." I said, "I got to."

I called Jill. She knew I would. She knew I was hooked and she was reeling me in. She told me about a cousin she wanted me to meet. I laughed and said, "That's bullshit and you know it. At least be honest with me about what you're up to."

We set a meeting up for that night at eleven o' clock at an all-night truck stop. I met with Jill and her cousin. It was ridiculous. Jill knew there was no way that her cousin and I were ever going to have any kind of date. Jill knew what she was doing; just getting me to come out so she could pull me in. She had felt jilted when we were younger and she had to settle her score. The three of us met and we sat and talked for over an hour. I was basically shaking my head at her the whole time.

The next morning, I received the call, "Could you meet me so we can talk?" I pleaded, "Please, just be honest. Damn it. You do not want to talk." Coyly she said, "Yes, I just want us to catch up." Defeated, I said, "Jill you know I am supposed to be at work already."

For all of about two minutes we were at the park where we met. I never even got out of my car. I just lowered the window and said, "Follow me to my friend's house." When we got to her house and were inside, it was like a scene from a movie, tearing at each other's clothes, kissing and going crazy.

I closed my eyes to kiss her and … all I could see were her two daughters and her husband. I cried. I could not do this thing with her. Not now, not this way. With all this sexual energy going on, I felt like I had been plugged into a wall receptacle and all I could think of was all the people that had helped me, all the guys I had helped get clean and sober, all the classes I had taught in ACIM and I was pissing on all of it. The guilt was more than I could bear. I could not perform for her. I tried to explain but she just laughed and said, "It will be different *next time*." She left and so did I.

I drove as fast as the old Buick would take me back to The Center. I packed my stuff, without saying goodbye to anyone and turned right back around to Kentucky and Jill, for the *next time*.

That energy was just way bigger than I was. I had no support, no meetings, no classes, no sponsor (that I was using), no Ed, no Callie and I don't think I had even been praying for a long time.

My thoughts were all over the place. 'How did I get here? What the hell was I thinking? She's married for God's sake. What about everything I said in *Taming the Dragon*? Ed and Callie will think I do not appreciate everything they did for me. Everyone will think that it was all a lie. Here I am again. What the fuck? God where are you? Please help me!' I was scared. I knew I was off track. I needed help. But … 'I wrote the book! I should know!'

I couldn't go into a meeting and ask for help. My pride was leading me right into the gates of hell. I knew it and still couldn't stop it.

I went to a friend's house, opened her fridge, pulled out a Busch beer and told myself, "Johnnie please put this down, you are an alcoholic and you have no business with this in your hand." I read the label, like I was looking for directions or something. Again I thought, 'Please put it down.' My soul was screaming, 'NO, DON'T!' I read the label again and then again.

I popped the top and the frost came seeping out of the opening. I felt like a metal ball being drawn to a magnet. I simply had to do it. It was just so much bigger than me. I told myself several times 'Johnnie you are an alcoholic.' It didn't matter.

I took the drink. I had heard the old-timers say, "The Twelve Steps may not open the gates of heaven and let you in, but they can certainly open the gates of hell and let you out." That is what they had done for me and now I walked right up to the gate, opened the door and stepped right back in.

Before I took that first drink, I still knew I was an alcoholic. Three beers a day … that was my quota. After successfully maintaining three beers a day for three days, the beast was already running the show. My thoughts became, 'Look at all the time you wasted in those meetings and all that work.' I actually got by with that three beer trick for about ten days.

One night I walked into one of my favorite old haunts and one of my old drinking buddies was sitting right inside the door. He had a pitcher of beer and was drinking from one of those little plastic cups. I had my three cups and thought, 'that is not hardly three beers.' Next thing I knew I had three pitchers and I was drunk.

When it hit me that I was drunk, I could not get to the restroom fast enough. I closed and locked the door and sobbed like a baby. Then I prayed, "God please get me home soon, I won't make it out here."

We have a saying in the meetings, 'There is nothing worse than a head full of Twelve Steps and a belly full of booze.' Truer words have never been spoken. I could not get drunk enough to turn the meetings and the sayings off in my head. Constantly the old guys from the meetings were conversing in my head and I could not shut them up. I drank like I had never stopped, still they kept on chattering, 'Nothing is so bad that a drink won't make it worse.' or 'One is too many and a thousand is not enough.' I would ask God, "How much will I have to drink to shut these guys up?"

In all my years of previous drinking, promiscuity had never been an issue, not from lack of effort, I was just usually too drunk to be available for sex. In this relapse, women suddenly noticed I had a pulse. They were everywhere. My self-loathing was back. This was not what I had worked for all those years. I had learned about dignity, integrity, and honesty. 'Where was "that guy"? What the hell happened?'

In the meetings we talk about the line that alcoholics cross from normal drinking to becoming an alcoholic. I never saw a line the first time and I certainly didn't see it this time but if there was a line, I had crossed it and all I could think was, 'How do I get back?'

The mental torment was excruciating. I was still seeing Jill. With a head full of Jack Daniels the guilt eased up enough for me to get through it without crying, at least until she left.

Three weeks into the abyss and I totaled the Buick. At seventy miles an hour I ran off the road and hit a tree. I broke my nose in so many ways it looked like an S. The doctor said there was no way he could fix it without major surgery.

After that wreck I crawled out of the ditch, found my way back to town, called a friend and asked him to come get me. He did but it took us a week to find the Buick. It was in a ravine so deep we couldn't see it from the road.

Drunk every day, I was still working every day and insistent on staying honest almost stupidly so. Jill's husband was a big man. It was a small town and people talk. Periodically someone would ask, "Johnnie, are you messing around with Jill?" I was afraid that if I started lying I would never find my way back. I would always say "Yes I am."

Eventually he found out about us. He told her that if he had been staying home instead of hanging out with friends that she wouldn't have needed to mess around with me and if she would quit, he would start staying home more.

She stopped seeing me. I was relieved.

After Jill there was Keri. I had known Keri from a meeting. She wasn't drinking with me, she just drove me around, no one wanted me driving after I totaled the Buick.

One morning I left Keri's house around two a.m. walking home, I had that old feeling of 'It's two in the morning and you are out here on the road, no one knows where you are and no one gives a shit.' Paul, an old gentleman I had known from the meetings popped into my head and said, "That is bullshit. There are any one of a hundred people you could call and they would come get you right now. You are out here now because you choose to be. You are no longer a victim to your addiction, this is your choice." I have a very visual mind. I could see him and the hurt in his eyes. He knew as I did, the life of drinking was no longer for me. I was humbled. So I prayed, as I did every night of that relapse, "God please get me home soon, I am not going to make it out here."

It had taken a few years for my grandmother to trust that my recovery was real but when she decided she could trust it she became very proud of me. Hung over one morning someone called and told me they were about to take her over to Missouri to an assisted living facility and that she had asked to see me before she went.

I went, trying to act sober. It was killing me inside that anybody who had been proud of me, no longer had anything to be proud of. Everyone was standing around talking and she was in the kitchen in a wheelchair by herself. She motioned for me to come to her and to kneel down beside her. Once there, she whispered, "If I get in trouble over there you are the one I will call for. You are the only son of a bitch in the bunch that can make me laugh." That was the last thing she ever said to me and the last time I saw her alive. At least she *thought* I was still sober.

Three weeks after I totaled the Buick my friend Mark and I stopped one afternoon after work for a beer, driving his grandmother's car. It was about four in the afternoon and Mark told me we couldn't stay long because he was already in trouble with his wife. I said "Okay, we will leave as soon as I lose my first game of pool." I lost a little after midnight.

By that time we were both very drunk and no longer cared about his wife. We weren't ready to stop when they closed the bar. Mark said he knew a young girl (nineteen) and that we could go party at her place.

I do not remember her name. I do however remember what took place. While we were sitting there drinking and smoking a joint, a couple from a church came to witness to her and try to help her straighten up. In the meetings if we go to help someone stop drinking, we call that a 'Twelve Step call'. *I* should have been there for a Twelve Step call instead of supporting this girl in destroying herself. If that didn't make me feel bad enough, what was coming would.

This was the night God decided to get me back home. *He sent a bus.*

When the couple came in I tried to ignore that whole scene. Some things are just inescapable. The girl looked at me at some point and like she had seen a ghost said, "Oh my God! You are Johnnie Calloway." I said, "No shit." The couple said, "He can't be Johnnie Calloway, he's drunk." I said, "Yes I am Johnnie Calloway and yes I am drunk." The girl said, "No you don't get it, you are Johnnie Calloway." The couple had brought her a copy of *Taming the Dragon* as an inspiration for her to stop. She held the book up and pointed at my picture on the back, "No! You are Johnnie Calloway the author of this book." And I responded, "I am tired of people confusing me with that asshole." My friend Mark interjected, "I am tired of you denying that is your book. Even though you are drinking again that was a great accomplishment for you."

The phrase 'lower than whale shit' came to mind.

Mark and I argued about who should drive. Neither one of us thought that either of us should be driving but we had to get home. We tossed a coin and I lost. Thirty minutes later I totaled his grandmother's Lincoln. This was the second car I had totaled in three weeks. And I broke my nose again. Funny thing about that is, it totally straightened out what the doctor had said would take major surgery to do. God can and will do for you what you (or a doctor) can't do for yourself.

By now it was about three in the morning. We were on a two lane back road in Kentucky. I was walking with my head held up trying not to bleed on myself, and a lady pulls over to pick us up. As I was getting in the car I said, "Thank you ma'am for picking us up out here. I appreciate your bravery since we are obviously drunk, obviously just wrecked that car back there and you don't know us." to which she responded, "I know you, Johnnie. You used to sponsor my husband."

I asked, "So what is lower than whale shit?"

CHAPTER 14

THE RETURN

I got up the next morning after the wreck, my nose full of blood, my shirt covered in blood and totally consumed by guilt and remorse. I had to be finished with this. I hadn't been up long before a friend came by to see if I wanted to go drinking. I said with little conviction, "I'm done." He knew I meant it. I actually think he wanted it to be so for me. He, (Mark) had watched my rise and my fall from a distance. Some think that drinking friends aren't real friends. Some are.

I bought a seventy two Chevy Nova from a friend. It had been sitting in a field for over three years. He said it was running when he parked it there and might still be running but it needed a battery, a wire connected, and four tires. Mark had four decent tires that he sold to me for ten dollars apiece. It had an old three fifty engine in it and it would fly.

Once again I was on the road for another personal growth adventure in another car that I wasn't sure had another twenty miles left in it. But I was certain that if I stayed in Kentucky I would drink again.

I worked a couple of days in tobacco and put together around seventy dollars. I hadn't driven the Nova enough to know what kind of gas mileage it got but again I had to go. The beast had tasted blood again with my relapse, and it was hungry.

I left Mayfield on a Friday morning headed for Sarasota, Florida...one thousand and ten miles away. During the relapse I had often talked to a sober friend in Sarasota about what was going on. He had asked me every time to come back to Florida and stay with him. After the second wreck I called and asked if that option was still on the table. "Absolutely.", he said.

So it was back to Florida and back to staying on someone's couch.

The drive back was grueling yet actually somewhat comical ... not at the time but in retrospect.

Just south of Nashville I did the math on my gas mileage and realized I didn't have enough money and gas to get to Sarasota. I turned around and headed back to Mayfield. After I turned back north I thought, 'Johnnie, if you go back to Kentucky you will drink again.' I turned back south, and then did the math again and turned back north. I made that loop four or five times before I decided that sober and without gas in Timbuktu Georgia was better than drunk in Kentucky.

I committed to Florida. I had a nice camera someone had given me in The Center that I traded for a tank of gas in South Georgia.

I arrived at Shaun's house in Sarasota on a Sunday morning with one dollar and sixty cents and a quarter a tank of gas. Shaun welcomed me with open arms and I stayed on his couch rent free for several weeks.

I was thirty-three years old. I had stopped drinking on November fifteenth, nineteen ninety one and left Kentucky on the sixteenth. I remember these dates because in the daily meditation book, *Twenty Four Hours a Day*, I read on November 18th about *procrastination*. I had planned on taking a few days to

149

breathe but after that reading, I decided to go look for a job instead of putting it off. I was hired on my first interview as a carpenter on a big remodel on Lido Beach, an island just off Sarasota. I worked there eighty plus hours a week. That job helped me to stay out of my head.

In the Twelve Step meetings we give out white poker chips or key tags to every new person that comes into the program or anyone who drank or used drugs again. We call that a relapse. I knew I had to deal with that humiliation in Florida where I had been a legend, at least in my own mind.

I was angry, disappointed, disillusioned and most of all ashamed. I went to a meeting right away, to face the music and swallow my pride. There wasn't much to swallow, there was no pride left. The first night back in Sarasota and I knew it was going to be one of the most difficult things I had ever done ... to walk back into a meeting and pick up that damn chip.

God was definitely playing His part and having His way. As I approached the door of the meeting one of my best recovering friends, Theresa, was standing outside. When she saw me she came running up to me and gave me a big hug, saying, "Johnnie I am so glad you are back in town, these young guys really need your recovery here." 'AAAAAAAAGH.' My gut churned, my eyes immediately watered, my heart raced and I just wanted to turn around and leave, never to come back.

After Theresa's statement, I thought, 'Let's see how you feel about my recovery after I pick up that damn chip.'

I sat through the meeting and never said a word, which was quite unusual for me. It is at the end of the meetings when the chips are given out. I had been met with a very warm welcome. Almost everyone in that room knew me and I knew almost everyone there. I think most of them liked me. I wasn't at that moment sure of anything though. But when I stood up and walked to the front of the room to get my chip, the room went church-mouse quiet and I didn't have a word to say.

There are some common things that we say to the person coming back from a relapse, "You didn't lose anything; Everything you learned is still with you; You aren't judged here; and We all just have today and time doesn't mean anything."

One of the things that I had been most grateful for (my first time around) was the fact that I was respected. What I had to say meant something. Prior to my relapse, when I started to share, if there were side conversations going on, they stopped. After my relapse, that was over and I was crushed. God was doing everything He could to assist me in the smashing of my ego.

Unlike what we had said, I *had* lost something, my credibility. Ed pointed it out to me but he also said, "You had to earn it the first time. You will have to earn it again. It might be a little tougher this time but you can do this Johnnie." I wasn't sure he believed that I could. How could he be? I certainly wasn't. There wasn't anything at that time that I was sure of.

Some of the people that I had thought were close friends avoided and shunned me. Again unlike I had been told, I *was* judged. Fortunately I understood what that was about and therefore I didn't take it too personally but it still hurt. My relapse frightened them, my vulnerability put their vulnerability in their face and they did not want to look into that mirror.

Ed had told me very early on in my first round of recovery, "Johnnie you are a full ticket." I asked, "What the hell does that mean?" He laughed, "If there is a Twelve Step program for it, you qualify." The truth is I did/do.

I therefore went to a few different types of Twelve Step meetings. In addition to the meetings that addressed my own addictions, I attended meetings for families of alcoholics, and ones for children of alcoholics. In one of them I had heard, "The ones that judge you don't matter and the ones that matter won't judge you."

We also say, "Stick with the winners." It didn't matter if I was being judged, shunned or if I had lost my credibility, I needed those meetings to live whether they needed me or not. I had to allow myself to gravitate to the people that seemed to be accepting me (usually the ones that had relapsed themselves). I had to suck up all the hurt and deal with it.

I was very uncomfortable in meetings for a long time. I do not know for how long now. It seemed forever.

After a few weeks at Shaun's, I found a friend who needed to rent out a room. Wow! I had a bed that I was paying rent on and not just using someone's couch. I started to feel like a part of society again.

After living there for about three weeks, I came home from work one evening and everything in the house was gone … *Everything!* The roommate, all the furniture, all the utensils, even the bed I was renting. There was only a milk crate left in the living room floor and it became my seat.

I cried. I didn't know what I was going to do. I stopped crying and asked God, "What should I do? Look for somewhere else to go? No damn it I am not moving again. This is going to be my home." I did not know the landlord, how much the rent was or even how to find the landlord. There was an antique store in the back of the house and I asked the man working in there if he might know who owned the house. He was the owner.

When my roommate left, he also turned off the electric, water and the cable. I told the owner what had happened. The roommate also left owing him money. I just told him the truth. "I want to stay here but all the utilities need to be turned back on and I need a few things. I cannot afford to give you first, last and security or the full four hundred a month. I can however, give you one hundred a week for a few weeks and then two hundred every two weeks until I get up to the four hundred." He decided to trust me and I had the first place that was *my* place, ever. I got the big room!

The job on the beach ended and I went back to air conditioning work. I started going to garage sales on the weekends, buying home furnishings. My first buy was a couch. *My couch!* I had spent most of my life on someone else's couch, now it was my couch. One afternoon after work and my shower I went in and laid down on the couch naked. All of a sudden I jumped up and thought 'You're not supposed to be on the couch naked.' Standing over the couch and looking at it, I realized, 'It is *my* couch. I can lay on the damn thing naked if I want to.' I lay on that couch and rolled around like a puppy on a blanket, naked.

A friend brought me a spider plant as a house-warming gift. I asked, "Why do you want to kill this plant?" I had never been good with plants. My dad had always been good with plants, not me. Soon there were plants all over the house (just like my dad). I started putting them outside as well and then I wanted flowers. I found some flowers that had tags on them that said 'Butterfly Attractor'. 'How cool, flowers and butterflies' so I planted several Butterfly Attractors from a local hardware store, to no avail. So I went to Barnes and Noble and bought a book *How to Build a Butterfly Garden*, learned how and became somewhat obsessed with the life of a butterfly. Today several of my friends call me "the Butterfly Guy".

It took a few months of getting my feet planted on the ground again before I went to a ACIM class. It wasn't long before I was facilitating again and in my home. The classes there were small, intimate and for ambiance the a/c was always down low with a fire in the fireplace.

I was facilitating rebirthings and re-enactments and doing some of my own. Helping others, I was starting to feel like I had value again. Facilitating the ACIM classes always made me feel good about myself.

One night after class one of the classmates told me I should have my own church. I laughed about it and told someone a few days later what he said. Soon after a lady (I did not know) showed up at my door and said she had something to show me. She was a realtor. She took me to a couple of places she thought I might be able to have a church. I went along for the hell of it, not thinking it would ever amount to anything.

She came by in less than a week and took me to another place. It was incredible! It was the oldest house in Sarasota, a beautiful two story house and next to it was the oldest church in Sarasota County. It was small and cozy, with lots of charm. They were historical buildings that had been moved to the same property. The pair made for a beautiful setting.

It turned out that I knew the owner and she was financially distressed. She couldn't get anyone to make use of those buildings. She was willing to do almost anything to turn a profit.

I had been bouncing back and forth between the two local metaphysical churches and leading the ACIM class. The idea, of what the center was to be, had taken on a life of its own. Not really knowing what was going on I just made it up as I went along.

I went to the two ministers of both churches and told them the plan that had occurred to me. I wanted to create a facility/center to bridge the gap between the two. "Both of you stand behind your podiums every Sunday and talk about Unity, I want to provide a space where the two can actually *be* that Unity instead of talking about it in our separate pods."

To say the least they were not impressed. The Unity Church Minister told me, "Johnnie that is a great idea. The bottom line is, this is a business. Every time he gets a member, I lose one." My heart sank. And I became even more determined.

My ACIM class helped me pass out fliers and promote a meeting at the little church on the property. The fliers basically said we wanted to start a Spiritual Development Center where *all* spiritual teachings would be embraced.

Before the first gathering I had three people willing to sit on the board. We decided it should be set up in the form of a club with paying members. It was presented in a "pot luck" dinner setting, very casual and very relaxed. I guided the group on a visualization of what the place would look like when it was open and going full force. We closed with me reading the last chapter of *Taming the Dragon*. By the end of that first night we had thirty five paying members and a full board of directors and a name, 'The Shanti Center.' Shanti is an ancient Sanskrit word that means *peace*.

The owner was wonderfully helpful. She allowed us to pay rent on a per-member basis. As the membership grew so did the rent.

In the beginning I was everything, the Director, the Founder, the Grounds Keeper and the maintenance man. I swept, mopped, kept books (poorly) and wrote all the promotional materials. The purpose of providing a space for unity to be experienced was happening. The place was full of life. In short order it was taking care of itself through its volunteers.

On Fridays, over eighty people would show up for our meditations that were followed by Spirit Dance. We were sometimes there until two or three in the morning. I continued to facilitate rebirthings and re-enactments. We had a massage therapist on site, a Reiki therapist, a spiritual counselor, an herbalist and many artists and craft workers providing their wares for the Shanti Center.

Almost everything was great. I was going to a meeting nearly every day, facilitating ACIM classes, running the Shanti Center and living my purpose. But I was battling periodic bouts of depression and suicidal thoughts. I wasn't talking to anyone about those. I wrote them off as just fear, and my old friends, *self destruction* and *unworthiness*. Not for one minute while I was at the head of the Shanti Center did I truly feel worthy of that position and I was frightened more often than not that I would be found out. The kid with a tenth grade education sat at the head of a board of directors that consisted of an attorney, a doctor, an accountant, a realtor and a bookkeeper, all constantly asking me what we should do. I was quite often concerned, 'Have I scammed them? Have I scammed myself?'

After a year and a month the Shanti Center was running out of steam and so was I. I had worked there for all that time and the most I ever made was three hundred and fifty dollars for one month. I had survived making money doing odd jobs for the members from the center. I had made a commitment for one year to the building of the center. I had exceeded the year and I was still broke and lonely.

At our final board meeting when asked, "What should we do?" My answer was simple, "We need to be done. Let's not go out like the old boxer that doesn't know when to stop and humiliates himself." No one argued. And the Shanti era of my life was over.

NORMAL

I no longer wanted to facilitate ACIM classes, rebirthings, re-enactments or chase anymore of the dragons that haunted me from my childhood. I did still want and need the Twelve Step fellowships. I just wanted to be a normal guy with a normal life.

A tool belt, a job and a girlfriend were what I wanted next in my life. I got the tool belt and the job right away. The girlfriend was going to take a while.

I was still in the neighborhood where I took over the place from the runaway roommate. The neighborhood was all old Florida homes being renovated and prices were sky rocketing. Everyone said the key to real estate was location, location, location. I discovered timing to be very important as well.

I had been helping Ed look for an investment property to purchase for quite a while when I walked past a place one day where an elderly lady was putting out a hand painted sign. I approached her and asked about it. There had been a realtor involved but according to the lady, they had been asking too much and it was taking too long. She was lowering the price (that morning). I called Ed, we set up a meeting with her and struck a deal pretty much immediately. A duplex and a triplex and I was a partner in a piece of property.

Ed made it a sweet deal for me. I couldn't have asked for a better situation. I had acquired credit as a result of actually working on one job for over a year and I had a brand new Ford pickup truck. Odd how every time I succeeded at something it felt like a victory over all those that said I'd never amount to anything ... and now I was partners in five rental units. A huge score for the home team!

Ed and I decided to take a trip to Kentucky. I think he wanted to see if all the wild stories I told him had any truth to them. There was one story in particular that he was really curious about. I had told him in my early recovery (the first time) that my dad once owned a Boston Terrier and how well house-broken the dog was. My dad had told the story that once after he had been gone for three days, as he was rounding the corner of the trailer, the dog was standing on the kitchen table pissing out the window.

While in Kentucky Ed got to meet my dad and without any provocation by me, he told Ed the story about the "window-pissing dog." Ed told me later that he always trusted me but that story had left him wondering. Now he knew I was telling the truth.

Jackie was in Kentucky with her twins while we were there. David and Amanda (Batman and Mando) were seven. Ed and I visited with them a few times. The kids really liked Ed and he enjoyed them as well.

We had a great time in Kentucky. It was the first time Ed and I had been on a vacation together, other than a handful of Twelve Step retreats.

My life was good. I was living the dream; no longer feeling the weight of the world or the responsibility to save it. The last eight or nine years had always had a sense of urgency to them. Now I could just breathe.

Soon after we returned from Kentucky, Jackie called. She was in trouble. She had been arrested for selling pot and it was a violation of her probation. She was in danger of going back to prison and losing her kids. If there was anything I could do to help I had to try.

Ed and I decided to let them come live in one of the units we had remodeled. I knew I was going to have to play the dad role. There were a few things I knew about kids (from being one for thirty years). I knew they were going to test me to see how far the rope goes, I knew that consistency was vital and discipline was needed. I was going to have to make them my priority. I did and I enjoyed it very much.

The kids loved to wrestle in the yard. I got to be a kid with them but we had rules. If I had to scold them sometime during the day, no one went to bed without taking a walk with me. On the walk we would talk about what they were scolded for and they could ask Uncle Johnnie questions. At first they did not like the walks or the talks. Soon though, if they thought we weren't going to take the walk, they would come get me. "Uncle Johnnie we haven't had our walk yet." It was so cool. I think I was parenting myself through them.

We went to the park often. The rule for the park was that there was a predetermined amount of time that we would stay. It was either thirty minutes, forty five minutes or an hour. But if they went the entire time without having to be scolded they got to play an extra fifteen minutes. If they got in trouble they lost fifteen minutes. After a while if one of them saw the other start to do something they shouldn't, one would call the other down and I wouldn't have to. It was usually Amanda keeping David in line. She was like his second mother.

After eight months Ed and I sold the property. We made a great profit for the short time we owned it. It was more money than I had ever dreamed of having. I wanted to help Jackie and the kids so Jackie and I decided to open a booth at the Red Barn Flea Market in Bradenton, Florida, just north of Sarasota. Jackie, the kids and I went all over the state looking for special products for our booth. I put a big portion of my share of the money from the property sale into the flea market (about forty percent). It was a struggle starting off but it was picking up. We had our booth there for about ten weeks when ... the entire market burned to the ground. In the flash of an eye the whole thing was gone.

I asked, "Really God? I have got to start over from scratch, again?" I felt the blow from that one pretty deep but I had gotten really good at just getting back up. This time I had two kids looking to me for how to handle adversity. Being a good example to them meant everything to me. This time was tough. I thought I was set for life with the amount of money I had made on the property and in just a few months it was almost gone.

The places were sold and I had my sister and two children looking to me for a home. I did have some money left and there was always air conditioning for me. We got a place right around the corner from where we were and I got a job.

I think Ed was heartbroken for me about the loss of everything. He introduced me to his good friend Neecy (Denise Goldman). That relationship didn't turn out to be what Ed had hoped for but she and I became great friends. She helped me out a lot with the kids.

When the kids came to me, David was going through that little boy stage of making up these incredible stories and swearing they were so. I looked at it as him exercising his imagination in a very creative way. I tried to explain the importance of people being able to trust you if you told them something and he got it.

When he would tell me one of his elaborate fabrications, I would ask, "David are you exercising your imagination or is this something I need to believe?" Most of the time he would roll his eyes, sigh and say in his thick southern accent, "I'm exercising my imagination Uncle Johnnie." Once after hearing one of his elaborate tales, I asked the question. He really huffed this time and said, "I'm exercising my imagination Uncle Johnnie, but would you work with me here?"

After we lost the booth at the market and moved, I came home one day to find Jackie smoking pot on the porch. I was enraged. I told her she couldn't smoke pot in my house. I had worked too hard to make a name for myself and to clear that stuff out of my life. I could not take the risk of an arrest in the house. She decided to go to West Virginia.

I wanted the kids to stay with me. David said, "Uncle Johnnie I know you want us to stay, but she needs us. She's my mom. I want to stay but I can't."

While they were all with me it truly felt like I had family. For the first time I felt like I should have been a dad, that I wanted to be a dad and that I would have been a good dad.

Once they were gone, I fell into a real funk. I had a hole in my heart and I needed something to fill it. A friend of mine was meeting women on the internet and dating a lot. 'The right woman would fill this hole in my chest.' I wanted to learn how to date, I had never done that.

What I was doing on the internet wasn't dating. It was hooking up, a different woman two or three nights a week. It wasn't even fun and I could feel my soul corroding away. My self-loathing was returning. It was as addictive as drinking or drugging and I knew that if I continued in this way I would eventually drink and if I drank again I would die the lonely death of an alcoholic. I really just wanted to be normal.

I lost any ambition that I had for spiritual growth. I just wanted to find *the* girl and grow old with that special someone like everyone else seemed to be doing. I was not going to find *the* girl on the sites that I was cruising. Most of the women were married and just wanted to have sex. I was a single, healthy male and I often justified that what I was doing was natural and that most single men would be okay with what I was doing ... *I* was not ok with what I was doing. I won't say that what I was doing was wrong but it was wrong for me. I had learned while in The Center, 'There is no right and wrong, just right and not right for me.' I had spent years already trying to become a better man and I was not *being* that man.

I lost it all ... again. I moved in with Neecy. The internet hook ups had become another head of the beast (an addiction). I knew I needed to stop. It was not working for me to stay with Neecy either. She had become a good friend and it was too difficult for her to watch me in one of my addictions.

Another friend found a place next door to her for me and I moved in there. I was still going to meetings but I was no longer very active in the groups. I was just existing. I had to stop the internet hook-ups.

Then I met Stephanie, a relationship of convenience. I used her to get away from the internet games. I wanted out of the life I had trapped myself in and I knew that if I was in a relationship I would be faithful. I always had been. In all my insanity, infidelity had never been an issue. Stephanie would be my way out. She was married but sleeping on the couch, just waiting for the opportunity and the means to leave. I provided both and moved her in with me. I barely even knew her.

CHAPTER 16

THE HOME(S)

By this time I was forty-years old and seven years clean and sober (the second time around) and living with a stranger. We moved into a garage apartment and I was back into air conditioning. I was making pretty good money and things were going well. I was no longer doing the internet hook ups. Stephanie's presence had accomplished what I had hoped.

Neecy called me one day crying and told me I had no idea how I had hurt her. She had wanted more from our relationship than I could give her but she had hoped that I would change my mind. I hadn't. It hurt me to the core to know that she was hurting like that and it was because of me. When I got off the phone I turned around, looked at Stephanie and asked her to marry me. She said, "yes" and we were engaged. I had now known her for about a month or maybe two.

Soon after the engagement we saw an old neighbor of mine from the rental property I had owned. He told me of a new neighborhood he was in that was 'up and coming' and the house across the street from him was for sale.

My credit was gone but my name was still good. The house was owned by someone I knew from the ACIM classes. He chose to overlook my credit rating and trust my word. He gave me a great deal.

We bought the house with the stipulation that it would be in my name. We all agreed and I was a property owner again. Wow! The boy from nowhere Kentucky owned a home again. All I could think of was my dad and the fact that, to my knowledge, he never even owned a car.

This time it was *mine*. I could do with it as I wished. Stephanie and I set forth to make it a home. It was a beautiful old Florida house with lots of character. We both liked the Key West style for the color and the quaintness. We made the entire front yard a butterfly garden with a Koi Pond ... a little piece of Heaven. After the first year by three o' clock the front lawn was full of butterflies. I loved coming home to the sound of the waterfall and seeing butterflies everywhere.

Often when I would come home there would be a complete stranger sitting on the front porch taking in the tranquility of the place. The first few times this happened it was a little scary. The beauty and peace of it was just too compelling. I decided it was a compliment and the strangers probably needed the experience of sitting in the wonder of it. God had given me the talent to create this place and I owed it to those who could enjoy it to share it with them. The pond was surrounded by angel figurines, cherubs and other lawn art. It was brought to my attention many times that the art could be stolen. This place was a labor of love and it was obvious that it was special. Nothing was ever stolen from the yard but several items were left on the porch to add to the beauty.

There were many Hispanic children in the neighborhood. Most of them called me Mr. Johnnie. One of the children in particular loved to help me clean the filters to the pond and collect the chrysalises for the butterflies. Frequently he would come by and ask if we could clean the filter or if he could bring a friend over to see what a butterfly egg looked like. Sometimes we would clean the filter even if I had just cleaned it.

I started having ACIM classes in the house and going to 'Clearmind' Workshops that were being held in the area. The re-connection with Callie through Clearmind and a whole new group of ACIM friends was very uplifting for me.

With Clearmind and Duane O'Kane, rebirthings and the re-enactments became a part of my healing process again. I had wanted to believe that all that was over for me. The scars from my childhood and my life ran very deep and I had no idea how much they still ran my life.

I was taking butterfly chrysalises to the weekend workshops to represent the metamorphosis that each person had gone through. The butterfly release was very symbolic of the transformation each had experienced. I truly loved being a part of another's healing process.

Stephanie on the other hand, seemed to be greatly disturbed by the whole thing and wanted nothing to do with any of it. We hadn't been good together to start with but as I got more into my *purpose* and my *path*. It seemed like she resented it and me.

She began to participate, reluctantly. During one of the weekends Stephanie became angry with a lady and made a scene. I made the mistake of taking the other lady's side. That night I woke up with Stephanie standing over me with this look in her eye … a look that was all too familiar to me. It was like no one was home in her eyes and I was afraid. I knew then that I needed out.

I was doing well with air-conditioning and taking periodic trips to Kentucky. I even bought a duplex and I had a home and another rental property. I was on my path back to being a responsible and productive member of our society.

Before leaving for one of my trips to Kentucky, Stephanie mentioned that if something happened to me on the trip, the state could take everything and neither she or my family would get anything. It all would be lost. She knew about real estate so I asked, "What can I do to protect myself?" Her response was, "You could give me power of attorney." The next day we did just that.

Our fighting progressed and I just couldn't take it anymore. One morning I told her that I was done, that I would sell the two places and give her half of everything. She could stay at the house and I would find some place to go because I knew that would be easier for me than it would be for her and I left.

All hell broke loose. There had already been people looking at both properties and selling them would be easy and very profitable. The day I left, Stephanie went directly to the courthouse with the power of attorney to file a lease option on the house and a quit claim on the duplex.

I spoke with a gentleman who had expressed interest in the duplex and we came to agreeable terms. The day before we were to close he called me and asked about Stephanie's name on the deed. My reply was, "Her name is not on the deed." Yes it was.

I had been hopeful that it could be an amicable end. Now a war had ensued. Stephanie, who I never even married, took my entire sentimental property hostage; my photos of my mom, my baby book, my book of poems, a pocket watch that Jackie had bought me, and a black and white photo of a barn that Ed had taken while we were in Kentucky. She swore she knew nothing of them.

Now an attorney was needed and it got ugly. I moved back into Neecy's temporarily. Stephanie set out to destroy everything that meant anything to me. She went to Neecy and told her things I had said in an attempt to destroy that relationship. Fortunately honesty had me share the truth with Neecy all along. Everything Stephanie shared with Neecy, she already knew. Neecy had to call the police to get her to leave her house.

Ed, my attorney and my doctor suggested I go to Kentucky and give her time to calm down and time for *reason* to come to her.

Before I left for Kentucky the last thing Ed said to me was, "Johnnie go meet yourself a good little country girl." I always did whatever Ed said!!!

On the way to Kentucky I stopped periodically to call back and check on things. Stephanie had called Neecy and told her that if I didn't come back and sign the papers, she would have my cat put to sleep. Fluff was an outside cat and my friend Jim went by and rescued Fluff and took her to Neecy's. Fortunately I had my nine pound Papillion, Polly with me and she was safe. When Stephanie discovered that Fluff was gone she tried to get me arrested for stealing Polly. Polly was registered in my name, and Stephanie didn't have a leg to stand on for that one.

I was an emotional wreck. Once again everything was at risk. I didn't know if I had it in me to start one more time from scratch. Jackie had bought a house in Kentucky and I stayed with her once I got up there.

I needed support and went to a Twelve Step meeting to find it. Polly went with me. She went everywhere with me. Even though she only weighed nine pounds she went with me to work. The guys on my jobs used to laugh about the little dog on the jobs with the pit bulls. The two of us were quite the pair. I was the recovering redneck who raised butterflies and had a Papillion.

That night in Paducah Kentucky, I met Karen. She was beautiful and very sweet. But ... she was married. That definitely made her off limits. Damn! After the meeting she spotted Polly in the van and came running, wanting to pet her. Polly wanted nothing to do with her and actually tried to bite her. That tiny Papillion trying to bite anything was a sight but she had a major reaction to Karen.

Once Jackie heard the story of Polly's reaction to Karen her response was, "Son (anytime Jackie started off with 'son' I knew she was serious), I do not know this woman or anything about her but you had better listen to that dog." I laughed and wrote it off as Karen had just startled Polly. Besides it didn't matter anyway, she was married.

Going to meetings every day, as usual, I was starting to feel grounded again. Karen was at most of them too. One night after a meeting, we were chatting and she asked if I wanted to go with her and a friend for coffee. Coffee after a meeting is something that is very common in the fellowships. I felt it was okay since she had a friend with her.

She told me about her situation with her husband. He was abusive, both emotionally and physically. They were separated but she was still living in the same house with him, and sleeping on the couch. He knew that as soon as she could she would be leaving. She just needed a place. I still felt everything was okay. I was going back to Florida.

She asked if I would help her find a place. I did and I loaned her half the money for the move. Now I had crossed the line. I was still emotionally shaky from dealing with Stephanie and the mess in Florida. Karen's presence was making that easier to deal with. In my mind Karen was the reason I came to Kentucky and made it all make sense. The troubles with Stephanie had to happen to get me back to Kentucky to meet Karen. It was all part of God's plan. Even Ed had said, "Go meet a good little country girl." I just had to follow his direction.

The very day that Karen moved into the trailer, the sex started and I was off to the races. Prior to that day I truly believed I was just helping a lady out who was being abused. I still believe that to some degree.

Postponement after postponement kept me from returning to Florida. Not wanting to have to deal with Stephanie was a huge part of that. Her anger had only escalated since I left.

Thirty days after meeting Karen, I asked her to marry me, while still breaking up with Stephanie.

I wanted family again. I still missed being a father figure to David and Amanda. Karen had two children. We got married as soon as her divorce was final. I had totally ignored Polly's warning, Jackie's warning, even Karen's mother's warning and the fact that she was only thirty four and I was going to be husband number *seven*.

The day of our wedding Karen's mom called me to the side and whispered, "Son, I hope you know what you are getting into." I told myself she was 'playing', but really knowing she wasn't.

I was no longer making my decisions. I was totally in react mode, running as fast as I could to avoid feeling what was going on in Florida, terrified of the process of starting over again, but at least now with Karen and her children there would be family again.

We needed to go back to Florida and settle my affairs there. I had to change attorneys because the first one said, "Johnnie, buddy this is going to be too grueling of a fight. I need to step down and turn you over to someone that is better prepared for this kind of case."

My new attorney felt very confident that we could win the war. Stephanie was not pulling any punches. She tried to have a restraining order put on me, to no avail. We went to the trial for the order and I had eight character witnesses (from my Twelve Step family). She was alone and I actually felt sorry that she had no one to stand with her. The judge dismissed the case.

She continued to deny knowing about my sentimental belongings. Karen and I were staying in a condo that belonged to a friend of mine. Stephanie called one afternoon and left a message on the answering machine, "If you want those things you are missing (and she itemized them), you need to come by the house and sign these papers, or you will never see them again." That was the wrong thing to do, with Karen listening. Karen called her back immediately, "You dumb bitch. Did you seriously just leave a message on this phone stating that you do in fact have the property that you have been denying even existed? Now you have thirty minutes to leave all those things on the porch so we can pick them up." Thirty minutes later everything was on the porch. Stephanie had met her match.

My first attorney had told me early on about taking over the house by going in while Stephanie wasn't there and changing the locks, because the house was in my name she could not make me leave. One day that is exactly what Karen and I did. Fortunately while we were there, before Stephanie got home we loaded my valuables in my van (just in case).

When Stephanie got home the van was in the back of the house, the locks were changed and she couldn't get in. I was prepared for Armageddon and she didn't even flinch. She got on her cell phone, called the police and when they arrived she opened her purse and showed them an article of mail with her name and the address on it. The police officer promptly said to me, "Mr. Calloway we cannot make you leave, but we cannot make her leave either. Therefore you and your new wife can stay here with her or you can leave. My suggestion would be run." He realized in just a very brief conversation with her that for us to stay there would not be good.

We left, much to Karen's disappointment. Karen would have loved to have a fist fight with Stephanie.

A couple of months passed and my new attorney called me into his office. He had become a friend. He suggested that I try to settle with Stephanie after saying that there would be a ninety percent chance of us winning this battle but Stephanie could drag it out for as much as five years. "Meanwhile you will still be responsible for the mortgage." Then he asked, "What is winning? Johnnie as your friend and your attorney watching what you are going through, I hope for your happiness and your peace of mind, let this be over." I think she had worn down another attorney but I agreed.

I thought that settling with her would cost somewhere around twenty five to thirty thousand dollars. When the house was bought it cost fifty three thousand. I sold it three years later for one hundred fifteen thousand. The duplex was sixty two thousand and three months later sold for ninety five thousand, therefore leaving a profit before expenses to be around ninety five thousand. When Stephanie was done, I got thirty thousand. I took the money and ran.

Before Karen and I headed back to Kentucky we had a Florida wedding. All my friends loved Karen, even Sue, Ed's wife who had been very protective of me over the years. Her words about Karen were, "Johnnie I think you finally found the right one."

Back in Kentucky we lived with Jackie while we looked for a house to buy. I had come away from the situation with Stephanie with just enough money to put a down payment on a house, furnish it and buy a car.

We found a house to rent while looking for one to buy and to get us out of Jackie's hair. Sis and Karen weren't ever going to be friends. Jackie was just too suspicious of Karen. Karen went to work right away putting a wedge between Jackie and me. David and Amanda would come to visit when Karen's kids were with us. They all enjoyed each other's company.

I was working a lot and when I was gone Karen would put David and Amanda to work on the house doing her jobs. Of course the kids told Jackie and that stopped their visits with us. I didn't fight it. I thought it was best for the kids not to come. They shouldn't have been treated like the *help*.

We weren't getting along very well and the arguments started. Karen tried really hard to get me to hit her. I started to believe she was addicted to abusive relationships. It seemed that she did everything she could to make me hit her but I would just walk away. She had no respect for me because of that. She thought a 'real man' would give her a beating. She got me closer to the edge of that than anyone I had ever been around.

We bought a farm from her dad. A cute little four acre farm, and we had plans of making it a stopover for Twelve Step members on the road. The place was next to the interstate, which made it attractive for that purpose. We were envisioning a petting zoo, with cottages and a center for meetings and parties.

We were going through the money like there was no tomorrow. Jackie warned me not to put all my eggs in one basket. I thought she was trying to run my business and told her they were *my* eggs and *my* basket. She just nodded her head and sighed.

Karen continued to try to provoke me into hitting her and I continued to walk away. Then she started to be gone a lot and I never knew where.

We went to a Twelve Step meeting one night and the topic was the Ninth Step (the amends step). Once we were home from the meeting Karen sat up in the kitchen with a cup of coffee, which was very unusual for her. After a bit I went in to see what was going on.

She said that after listening to the meeting on making amends, she felt she needed to make amends to David. David, having been husband number five; the one she had a lifetime restraining order on because he threw her off a porch and broke both her legs. I said, "Now let me get this straight, he throws you off a porch, breaks both your legs and you owe him an amends?" She looked at me and said, "Johnnie you just don't know how good I am at provoking people." To which I responded, "Oh, hell yes I do. You just don't know how hard I am to provoke."

We went to bed angry. I did not sleep all night. Intuitively I knew the gig was up or at the very least headed in that direction.

The next day I cried most of the day at work. Thank God I worked under houses (duct work in Kentucky is under the house not in the attic). I decided to tell her that if lifting the restraining order on David was what she wanted to do then go ahead. When I got home that afternoon that is what I told her. She had already lifted it that day.

We were sitting on our back porch and talking when she said, "I'm done." I asked, "With this issue?" She replied, "No I am done with your ass. You have got to go." And I said, "Just where in the hell do you think I am going to go? You just wrote a check today for the last of our money and you have done everything you can to drive a wedge between me and my sister." She answered, "That crazy-ass sister of yours will always take you in. Go tell her what has happened and you will be okay."

I knew without any doubt whatsoever she would have called the law and said whatever she needed to get me arrested and a restraining order put on me. I left somewhat quietly and humbly drug myself to Jackie's to ask for help.

Once at Jackie's I asked her to take a ride with me. Jackie already knew what was up. She had seen it coming. I reported the afternoon to her and she said, "Well the little bitch is right about one thing. As long as I have a home you will have a home but little brother this one hurt. You chose her over me and the kids, and the kids are hurt. You and I will be okay but you are going to have to earn your way back into the kids' hearts."

Learning that you've been blind with your eyes wide open can be a difficult pill to swallow.

CHAPTER 17

THE AFTERMATH

Humiliation had become a way of life for me. I ran into everything head first, always hoping to find the one thing, person or substance to make me okay. This time I had been a total fool. Karen had played me from day one. The day we got married, the same day her mother warned me about her, Karen started pigeonholing money for her escape. She never intended for us to make it. While we were in Florida I believe she had an affair with an acquaintance of mine. She started seeing husband number five again as soon as we got back to Kentucky.

I discovered the husband before me (number six) had no idea she was leaving until after I helped her leave. He had thought everything was just fine. He had been blindsided and I had been part of it.

The same day I left she moved number five into the farmhouse. He soon became number eight, briefly.

Throughout my entire life I had never experienced anger the way I was experiencing it after she kicked me out. I would wake up in the middle of the night and fantasize about hurting the two of them. With all the hurt in my life I had never consciously wanted to physically hurt anyone but this time I did.

In the 'Healing Your Inner Child' work I had done, I learned tricks to help deal with anger; beating pillows with a foam bat, screaming as loud as possible and allowing myself to cry. Living with Jackie across from a freshly plowed field I would take a miniature baseball bat and beat dirt clods to powder, screaming and crying the whole time.

I was left with nothing. I had worked my rear-end off to have the few little things I had. In January of two thousand, I had sold two hundred, twenty thousand dollars worth of property and in June I had to borrow forty dollars to get my front tooth pulled and bum a ride to have it done. (I actually walked around for the next two years with that missing front tooth.)

I inventoried my anger just as I had been taught in the Twelve Steps and tried to forgive as I had been taught in ACIM. Yes, I was angry with Stephanie and Karen but I was enraged with myself.

I could not work. The air-conditioning job let me go. I was forty two years old and had nothing, again.

I hired an attorney. Karen hired an attorney and the fight began again, the second one in six months. I was worn out. A couple of months into the fight I called my attorney and asked if he had a pen and pad, then told him to write this down: "the microwave, my one hundred foot extension cord, my computer, my black and white barn picture and my tools. Call her attorney and tell him that is what I want, by Friday." My attorney was not happy, "Johnnie what about the car? It is yours and the money was yours from before the marriage. She has no right to it and the farm is yours." I said, "If I put those things on the list, the fight continues. I need it to be over. I can start over and get the stuff back but I am losing too much of my life fighting for stuff."

During this time my dad passed away. His passing was a beautiful experience, not because he passed but the miracle that happened as a result of his passing. They called us all and said he was going soon. When we got there he was fighting for every breath. I sat at the foot of the bed reading him his favorite passage from the Bible, Psalm 23.

Jackie was the miracle. She was standing at the head of the bed holding his hand, patting it like she would a child and crying. Almost whispering she kept saying, "It's okay Daddy, it's okay." He continued to struggle like he had something to say. He wasn't done yet. Then almost as if on cue, Jackie looked him right in the eye and said, "Daddy, *we* are okay." She had forgiven him and he needed to know it. As soon as she said it he took one last deep breath and was gone. It was beautiful. She had been terrorized by him throughout her entire childhood and she had forgiven him.

I started reading *A Course in Miracles* again from cover to cover. There are three hundred sixty five lessons (one for each day of the year) in the Workbook for Students of A Course in Miracles. I started and finished them again. I was constantly praying to be able to forgive Karen, Stephanie and number five/eight. I knew internally that my anger was killing *me*, not them. I had to find a way. I had forgiven my father for all the things he had done, surely I could forgive these people.

In ACIM I had learned that "Your true healing lies in identifying with your sameness." I did not want to find anything about myself that was anything like them. But it was there was, just as it had been there had been with my dad... the good and the bad.

I realized that now more than ever I was going to have to apply every spiritual tool that the Twelve Steps, ACIM and all the workshops had given me if I was going to make it. For sixteen years I had been preparing for this battle.

Ed was not around nor was Callie I would have to find a new mentor. I was still a wreck, reading, writing, talking to whoever would listen, doing anything I could not to act on the insanity going through my mind.

Violence was a part of my DNA and I had never acted on it. I had always been afraid of it. I had always feared becoming my dad. My anger had never been this intense. Forgiveness was my only way out. I knew what Callie would say, "Johnnie look for your sameness." My resistance to any part of me being able to do to someone what I felt had just been done to me, was really strong. I truly wanted to be the victim but I knew better.

Stephanie. How had I been cruel to her? I couldn't see it. Karen. How had I betrayed her? Nothing. Number five/eight. How was I like him? Had I been a thief in the night? ACIM, says, "Readiness is not mastery." I was not ready to see the truth but it was there.

I was going to two Twelve Step meetings a day if I could borrow a car. I needed somewhere safe and to be with people who understood.

I found a job on a chicken farm; one hundred eighty thousand chickens all under my care. It was the nastiest job I ever had and paid the least of any job I had for years. It came with a place to live and the owner had a car that he would sell me on a payment plan. I had to take it.

I started facilitating ACIM classes and doing everything in my power to see my part in all that had happened. My mind was not prepared as yet to suffer the humiliation of that truth. I knew without a doubt that I played a huge part and these people were only a mirror for my own short-comings and character defects but the truth was too much.

At a noon meeting one day, crying like a baby, I managed to utter out what was happening in my life. There was an older gentleman there. I could tell he was relating to every word I was saying. When I was through he said, "This will pass, Son. It may feel like a kidney stone but it will pass." I actually breathed a little sigh of relief when he spoke. I liked his candor and his wit. More than anything though, I knew he understood. Gerald was his name.

About a week later I saw him again. His humor and wisdom struck me again. I asked him if we could go to a meeting together. "Sure." He said.

Gerald quickly became a great friend and mentor. Almost every day we spent time together; meetings, meals or even just sitting in his yard. His wisdom was and still is reassuring, comforting and inspiring. Gerald was a simple man, incredibly intelligent but simple.

I have a book within me about all the little 'Geraldisms' he shared with me. They sustain me. He once said, "Wisdom is knowledge applied. Knowledge without application is just information." I have tried to apply all that Gerald, Ed, Callie and so many more have shared with me.

The chicken farm was a seven day a week job. Some were very short days but it was seven days a week. When that job was over I couldn't find another one right away. When I did, I told Gerald it was going to be difficult getting back into the swing of things. He said, "Don't worry son. It is just a rock thing." And then he went on to something else. He loved to lure me in that way. I couldn't wait to hear what he meant by this one, "Whoa, Gerald, what the hell is a rock thing?" "You never heard about the rock thing?" He asked with a smile. "If you have a big ole rock sittin' in the yard, it sits there just fine and if you want it to move it takes some effort. And if you have a big ole rock rollin' down a hill, it rolls just fine and if you want it to stop, it just takes some effort. This is just a rock thing Johnnie, a little effort and you'll be fine." That was Gerald, always drawing pictures with words.

Periodically my mind would return to the similarities between myself, Stephanie, Karen and number five/eight and what lessons were in there for me. I had been holding that truth down like someone neck deep in water trying to hold down pieces of Styrofoam. They were popping up too fast now for me to keep them hidden below the surface. The answers were not pleasant.

Sometimes ignorance *is* bliss. Often I wished I could just be a victim but my teachings wouldn't support that lie. It was so much easier to be the innocent bystander of random acts of insanity. But I had learned there are no victims. ACIM had taught me about my personal power and how I create my life. As much as I wanted to, I could no longer ignore my part in setting up these situations and relationships.

I was angry with each of them for doing the same things to me that I had done to them or others. But I started to see that they were my teachers and my mirrors.

Stephanie's cruelty was her wrong doing and I had held myself above that. In my mind I had not been cruel to her. Really? Was it not cruel to live with her for over two years under the pretense of loving her with the idea that we would marry? Knowing the whole time I was not going to marry her and as soon as I could find a dignified way to leave I would. Had I been honest? No, not at all.

With Karen, was it honest for me to ask her to marry me, knowing I didn't even know her. I ignored the warnings I had gotten from Jackie, her own mom, and even Polly? Hadn't

I used her as a Band Aid to get past the pain of my losses in Florida, just as she used me to escape husband number six?

Number five/eight: Had he done anything to me that I hadn't done to Stephanie and Karen's husbands?

The summation: I could not stand in judgment of them and make them wrong for doing some of the same things that I had done. We were all just looking for something to make it all better. I had learned, even before I wrote *Taming the Dragon*, that each person on this planet wants more than anything to be loved and simultaneously, it is what we fear the most. And there is always the 'Geraldism', "You better watch those stones you throw. Stones have a way of becoming boomerangs in mid-flight and returning to bop you in the forehead."

I started to feel out of place in Kentucky. No one understood (not even Gerald) a grown man who wanted to raise butterflies. The things that I had learned made me different and I could not feed my desire to grow there. My spiritual nurturing was missing. I loved Gerald. He was family to me. He once said, "Family is not determined by the blood that runs through your veins but by how you treat one another." Gerald was family. But he alone was not enough, and as for my biological family, they no longer knew me. They only knew the old me. They didn't seem to understand my need for the Twelve Step meetings or my ACIM classes.

The suicidal thoughts were coming back and I couldn't escape them. It was twelve miles between my house and Gerald's and on the way there I would often think of which tree I should drive into but once I got to Gerald's drive I was safe and I could breathe. Finally I shared my thoughts with Gerald about driving into a tree. His response was, "Johnnie I can't help you there. No matter how bad it got for me I never thought about leaving here. I can listen to you as long as you want to talk but I have no feedback. I know someone who does and if you want to talk to them I will take you there." His honesty about that matter gave me the freedom to speak the truth.

After the chicken farm, I got a job in a bucket factory. It was actually a plastics factory but I made buckets, for six dollars and fifty cents an hour. When I worked piece work in duct installation I often made fifty to sixty dollars an hour in Florida, so this was, to say the least a step down from that.

My pride was gone. I had nothing that I could wrap my mind around to be proud of and just 'not being a drunk' wasn't enough anymore. I was just *existing* again ... humbled beyond words... and there is a big difference between humble and humbled.

Ed's wife Sue, who had been a part time sponsor for me in my early recovery, was going around the country teaching basket weaving. She wanted to stop in Kentucky and see me. I was elated. I knew she would be a breath of fresh air. The plan was for us to go to dinner, and then she would stay that night at my place.

Sue has always been a 'matter of fact', take charge kind of lady. While she and I were sitting in my house chatting, she abruptly picked up the phone and called Ed, right in the middle of our conversation, "Ed I am sitting here with Johnnie Calloway. The only thing missing from his relapse is the drink. You need to get up here and get him back home." Three days later Ed was there to get me and what was left of my stuff.

On my way back to Florida (to Neecy's)... I was going home.

GRATITUDE

Somehow or another there had always been a degree of gratitude in my life (throughout all the chaos and loss) for God's Love in my life. In the roughest of times He was always there, not just after I quit drinking and drugging but always. God (I believe) was the voice I heard in the closet as a child saying, "There's more for you Johnnie, just hold on." That voice and those words got me through all the darkness ... that sometimes dim but always present hope carried me.

Now it was Neecy's turn to see me through the hard times. After Sue set it up for me to return home, I called Neecy to see if I could stay with her until I got a job and back on my feet. She never flinched. She rearranged her life to fit me in her small but comfortable home.

Upon my return to Florida I went to an old boss, Ernie, and asked for a job. He was more than happy to put me back to work. I had never done hourly duct installation. It had always been on the piece rate, which at the time seemed to be a thing of the past. I had no idea what to expect but he offered me eighteen dollars and fifty cents an hour. I was ecstatic. He could have gotten me for twelve.

At that rate I got on my feet pretty quick. I continued to stay with Neecy though. I think the extra funds were helping her out also. Plus we got along well and were great friends.

I was going to a lot of Twelve Step meetings, reflecting and still licking my wounds from the previous few years, taking periodic overviews of what my part had been in it all.

I still (purposely) hadn't replaced the front tooth from the Karen era. I used the missing tooth as a reminder to slow down every time I spoke to a female. I was very self conscious of it and there was no way I could open my mouth to speak without thinking, 'Johnnie, take it easy.'

After living with Neecy for a little over a year, my foot was run over by a forklift at work. I was really lucky that there were no broken bones but it mashed all the muscle and nerves. It was three months of physical therapy and surviving on a worker's compensation check and a lot of free time.

I finally reached a place where I was ready to get that tooth replaced. My friend David was a dentist. He gave me a *really* good deal and did a great job on it.

The worker's compensation people told me I would have a settlement coming and I started making plans for a business. While I was installing duct work, I had developed a process for duct installation where it was prefabricated, which made it much easier and faster to install while also saving a ton of material. I decided to devise a way of doing this for companies and implementing this in a way to save them time and money.

Once I got the settlement, my old boss Ernie became my first client. I have never thought of myself as a businessman therefore I have always taken on a partner for that part. I have just been the worker bee.

I had taken a female mentor for this round with the Twelve Steps. I thought I would be better served with a woman's perspective. I loved her and she became another great friend. Her husband was out of work and having a difficult time finding a job. He had experience in the business side of life. He was a great guy and he soon also became a very good friend and my business partner.

In short order we were doing a lot of business. I was training him in how to help me with the work but we could not keep up with the orders. We were working very long days together and really getting to know one another. I took no responsibility with the business end. I left that all to him.

We were paying me a lot of money. At least I thought it was a lot of money. What I didn't realize was we were paying me more than we could afford. My partner kept saying he wasn't taking anything for himself.

I was totally living in the space of gratitude. Things were great and finally I had found my place in life. Often I wondered how the money was working but I did not want to be bothered with that and I stuck my head in the sand. I just wanted him to take care of that and let me take care of sales and productivity. I was curious about how we came up with the cost and the price of our product but not enough to ask.

We managed to keep our heads above water for over two years (I believe). We got an investor and used some of the money and his credit to buy me a new Hyundai. I needed something reliable and good on gas for sales.

I moved into a nice condo and my life was better than it had ever been. My tooth was fixed but still there was no woman in my life. There were periodic dates but nothing lasting. The perfect woman was the only thing missing.

We had hired a couple of guys to work the shop so I could be in the field being our salesperson. I was having time to play.

I was going to the gym every day, sometimes twice a day. I was healthier and leaner than I had been since The Center.

I was going to a noon Twelve Step meeting every day, mainly just to be with my people. One day I spotted a lady at the meeting I had never seen before. She was small and well built (okay she was hot!) and looked like she had just come from the gym. After the meeting she got away before I could introduce myself.

I went back the next day hoping to see her again, and there she was. I took the risk of making a fool of myself (no big task) by motioning to her before the meeting started to meet me outside once it was over. She simply nodded her approval.

After the meeting several people were almost lined up to talk to her and I just waited my turn. When everyone else was gone, I stepped up to her and she handed me her business card and told me she was going out of town for a couple of days for a 165 mile bike ride. She would be back on Tuesday so I could call her then.

I couldn't wait to tell Neecy. There was something about her that was different. I almost wished my tooth was still missing. I knew I was going to have to keep myself in check. I was having a difficult time waiting until Tuesday. Neecy kept saying, "Go ahead and call her." I was determined to wait and I did but on Tuesday I called.

Her name was Valerie and as soon as she gave me her card I put her name in my phone. The next couple of nights we spoke on the phone for an hour or so each night. There was good chemistry between us.

She discovered right away that I was well respected in the Twelve Step community. The third day I had gone to the noon meeting hoping to see her. She wasn't there. Five minutes after the meeting my phone rang and it was her name on my screen. My heart raced and I thought, "She's calling me, Woo hoo!"

She sounded frightened though and said there was something she needed to tell me and she needed to tell me right away before someone else did. She asked how soon I could meet her. I was free for the afternoon and said, "Whenever you want." I was truly bummed out. I just knew she was going to tell me she was married or had an out of town boyfriend. Many other thoughts ran through my head that were going to make her off limits.

We met thirty minutes later at Island Park by Marina Jack's in Sarasota. When I arrived at the park she was already waiting for me at the entrance. I was prepared for the worst, thinking 'Well that was short lived.' I had no idea what was coming.

We walked to the back of the park and she asked me to sit. She continued to stand and looked somewhat nervous. She said, "Last night when I got off the phone with you I thought, 'this is a really good man' and then I got scared. I realized there are some things about me that you really need to know and you need to find them out from me and no one else." I am still thinking, "Okay who is he?" She continued, "If this thing with us is going to go anywhere you need to know I have HIV and I have had for over twenty years. I am very public about my status. Everyone who knows me knows I am HIV positive. If people start seeing us together they will assume you are positive also and people can be very mean. I know this is scary. Even if you are okay with the risk, you know I may die someday." She paused. Her sincerity was overwhelming, her caring, her courage and her honesty were like a big fish hook that just pulled me in. At that moment she could have told me her lips were poisonous and if I kissed her I may die on impact and I probably would have kissed her anyway. No one had ever been that honest with me and took that kind of risk with me. Stick a fork in me I'm done!

She went on telling me about how I would have to educate myself about HIV and the risk involved, how to protect myself, how I could find everything I needed to know on-line and where to find it. The truth is, I was relieved that she wasn't married. Maybe I was just too ignorant about what HIV really was but I didn't care.

My mind was racing. 'How can I help? What can I do? Is she real? Was she really that caring of me without even knowing me? And I realized, this wasn't about her caring for me, she didn't know me. She was just being true to her own integrity. She would have done this for any other human being.' And the hook just went deeper.

When she was done, she stood over me and just looked into my eyes as if she were trying to see my thoughts. I was stunned not in the way most might have been. 'who she was' stunned me. Then with much trepidation she said, "If you get up right now and walk away, I will understand. Others have done just that. I know this is big and scary and it is a huge risk."

Again my mind was racing with, 'You think this is a risk? We are all going to die someday. I have placed my heart, my soul and everything I've owned on the line for women that couldn't have been that honest with me in a million years.'

It was my turn to speak, "Are you kidding me? Listen lil' girl, as far as dying goes I could get run over leaving this parking lot and I have dealt with death my entire life. I could go before you do. As far as me walking away, it isn't going to be that easy. You couldn't run me off right now with a tank. I have looked for that kind of honesty and integrity for twenty years. I am not going to just walk away from it now that I have found it."

That was January twelfth, two thousand and six. I had fifteen years without drugs or alcohol. Val was just about to have nineteen years.

I went on-line and learned as much as I possibly could about HIV. I couldn't wait to tell her all that I found, thinking I could tell her some things she didn't know, not realizing this was her life. She had to study this thing for her survival and she went around the country teaching others about HIV. To say the least she was amused by my enthusiasm.

The honeymoon was on and everything was perfect. My life was better than I had ever dreamed it could be. I owned a thriving business, lived in a nice condo, drove a new car, had great friends and a beautiful new girlfriend.

Val warned me that she couldn't handle neediness. I told her it could be an issue for me but I would work on it and straight away went back to therapy. I down played it and just hoped working on it would get me past it.

This relationship was so entirely different for me. She didn't need me to rescue her, to provide for her or to pamper her. She just wanted a partner. I had no idea how to be a partner or how to trust love.

Without realizing it I was subconsciously looking for reasons *not* to trust her. She gave me none. I knew how to be with the untrustworthy, I knew how to be with the uncaring and the selfish and I knew how to be with a child needing to be coddled. I did not know how to be with Val.

I had reached a place (I thought) where I was okay just being Johnnie. With Valerie all of a sudden I was not enough. I needed to change the way I talked. My accent and not using proper English didn't work. I began to pronounce "ing" when needed instead of just "in'." I even asked her to help me because now that I was with her I was going to work harder at being a public speaker. I began to dress differently, to talk differently and to change the person that I and many others had known. In retrospect, I abandoned myself.

One afternoon in the midst of all this perfection, driving to my business partner's house, I had a panic attack. In all my years of living in chaos and calamity, I had never had a panic attack. When I got to his house I ran into his second bedroom, jumped on the bed, buried my face in a pillow and sobbed like a baby. I had no idea why.

Even with all this wonderful stuff going on I lost sight of all that I had to be grateful for. I wasn't enough, I didn't have enough, I didn't know enough and I was not good enough. I was terrified. I convinced myself of all of this and the terror just kept growing.

The neediness became so overpowering that I couldn't escape it. It was humiliating to the point of being demoralizing. The things I did to control Valerie were embarrassing to me and my confidence dwindled to nothing.

The gratitude was gone, the honeymoon was over and the nightmare was coming.

CHAPTER 19

THE NIGHTMARE

I had always had bouts of depression and suicidal thoughts and accepted them as a part of life, but never like this. The anxiety and depression were crippling. The things I did to help me cope were extremely ego deflating. When I met Val I was at my peak … strong, confident and self assured but in a very short time that was all gone.

I moved in with her very quickly. I had taken in a roommate and I asked Val if I could stay with her for a while until he found a place. Quickly my things began to show up at her apartment. The next thing she knew I was a permanent resident. I was terrified of losing her; living with her would help me feel safer.

I stopped participating in my business. My partner and his son took over. They didn't know the business as I did so things started falling apart. There were many things going on there, that if I had been a part of, may have played out differently. But I needed to be with Val to make sure we were alright.

I finally went to a psychiatrist. The crash was coming fast and I needed help. Thus began the medication fiasco. I often felt that my doctor was guessing or throwing darts at a board to decide which medication I needed. He had a very difficult time finding my 'cocktail'. Actually, that doctor never did find it. Over a year passed while I was being rotated from one medication to the next looking for the right mix. Some of the attempts actually made me feel crazier.

My first time at the doctor's office while waiting, I read a pamphlet on panic attacks. The thing that stuck with me more than any of it was "The fear of panic attacks will only create more panic attacks." That was like saying, "Don't think about the color of your car."

Living with Val was not what I had hoped for. Val was a lot neater and cleaner than I was and she was strong enough to express her thoughts. I was already terrified and adding this to the mix made 'walking on egg-shells' an understatement.

In all my relationships, trying to please my partner had been my focus. If I performed well enough they might stay, even the ones that I didn't want to stay.

With Val, that was intensified. I hated it, but she was playing the role of my mom. I climbed right up on the chair and started drying dishes or standing beside the bed folding towels, except now I did it with a hammer or a shovel; fixing things, doing projects around the house and yard. I was trapped psychologically, as the five year old trying so hard to do whatever it might take to keep Momma from leaving. The ego deflation I was experiencing was beyond words.

Fear ran my life and I didn't know why. I was absolutely powerless over my neediness and it did not matter what Val did to help. She was helpless and she knew it but that didn't stop her from trying. I was watching what she was going though and knew it was due to my behavior. I was paralyzed by thoughts of her leaving and with guilt that I could not "man up" and do the right thing (leave or go do my work). As my fear of losing her increased the more frequent the panic attacks and the depression came upon me.

I do not think there are words in our language that can describe the physical agony that came with that level of depression. My stomach hurt all the time. I could feel in my head every heart beat pounding like my temples were being tapped with a small hammer. It was agonizing and I could not escape it. I felt like my body was running ninety miles an hour and my feet were nailed to the floor.

In my mind Val was my answer. If I could just make her happy it would all go away but the pressure of that became too intense. Part of my mind knew that belief was absolutely insane but my mind and logic were no longer in charge. I was on auto-pilot and fear was the pilot.

I ended my business partnership. I think my partner was watching my demise and was relieved when I told him we would no longer be working together.

I could not sleep. When I would go to bed before Val, the concern for what she was doing and why she wasn't in bed with me consumed me. I knew there was no reason for me to be afraid but I had no control over my behavior. I would get up and try to force her to come to bed. I was angry and terrified all at the same time. Eventually she would come to bed, angry over being manipulated and controlled.

The fear was like being in bed with my dad. I would not move. I tried to breathe in her breathing pattern trying not to disturb her. The anxiety was overwhelming and I simply could not sleep. Sleep deprivation was taking me down fast. The fear of going to sleep was overwhelming but the fear of waking was even worse. I knew when I was awake the suicidal thoughts would consume me.

My suicidal thoughts were constant. I could not find a safe place to escape from them. Even my Twelve Step meetings, which had always helped me feel safe, weren't working. Talking to anyone who would listen, I told them how much I wanted to take myself out. I was watching people lose their respect for me. Being respected by my peers had been a barometer of my success. Now respect was slipping away and that only added to my depression.

I had become this frightened little boy that wanted everyone to feel sorry for me and make me feel better. No one or nothing was working. I would scream at God, "Where the hell are you? Why have you abandoned me?"

In my ACIM training I had summed up some of the teachings to say, 'Nothing happens to me, everything happens for me. Everything is a gift.' Therefore in some of the darkest times I could wrap my mind around the thought no matter how briefly … 'Someday Johnnie you will see this as a gift.' Also, 'Just hold on Johnnie there is more for you.' These were brief but they got me through.

Val came home one day to find me in the fetal position on the living room floor, rocking myself and sobbing. I spent hour upon hour in that position and the crying was constant. She came over to console me as best she could and I asked her, "Just how much pain is a person supposed to endure to keep someone else from hurting?" What I meant by that was, at that point the only thought keeping me from pulling the trigger was her finding me dead and how it would affect her and what kind of message that would be sending to those who had helped me, and those I had helped. Quitting was not the legacy I wanted to leave behind. I thought of all my nieces and nephews frequently, 'How would my suicide affect them?'

After I parted ways with my business partner, I started the company back up under a different name. I had nothing for it though … nothing. I could not function. The bottom fell out of the economy. The need for my type of services went with it.

Unfortunately Val had believed in me and the idea that my business would make it. She had loaned me a very large sum of money to make it work. It didn't work.

After it shut down I got a job. I was literally coming unglued. I couldn't hold a thought for more than twenty seconds and couldn't see any thought through to completion. I had done duct installation off and on for twenty seven years. At my job one day after taking all my tools off the truck, I walked to my ladder and panicked. I walked around the ladder several times crying. Not knowing what to do, my entire body was vibrating, my eyes were twitching, my heart was racing and felt like it was going to pound out of my chest. I sat down on that job and cried like a two year old. The entirety of whatever self worth I had was always wrapped around my job performance or my performance for the *one* in my life. I was failing miserably at both now. Walking around that ladder, not knowing what to do was a punch in the stomach that was difficult to overcome.

Somewhere in this abyss I had revised and republished *Taming the Dragon*. Now on this job with my mind racing I thought with all my panic driven insanity, "This is God trying to tell me that he wants me to spend time promoting my book." I called my boss and told him I wasn't feeling well, that I would finish the job the next day and went home. Tomorrow would be another day.

Next day back on the job, the same thing happened. This time though, I convinced myself this was God getting my attention. I called the boss, told him that God wanted me to quit the job. I did not do as good a job convincing myself as I thought. I could not tell Valerie the truth. I lied and you can never tell just one lie. I said, "They no longer needed me. There wasn't enough work."

For twenty two years I had been doing everything in my power to be honest and live with integrity and I had just lied to the person that meant the most to me. My spiral down started to pick up speed.

One story then another to cover up the last and eventually Val put it all together and it didn't add up. I saw the light go out in her eyes when she realized I had lied to her. She had always said that the thing she loved the most about me was she could always count on me for the truth. That was gone and that deeply affected us both.

After quitting the job and on the decline, one day Val said, "I have accepted that you cannot work. Can you just help me around the house?" I said, "Of course." I even asked if she would stay with me if I went on disability.

She would leave to go to work leaving me with a dryer and a dishwasher to empty. I could not make up my mind which needed to be done first and would collapse on the floor or on the bed, paralyzed by indecision. At no time in my life had I ever felt so worthless and absolutely useless.

The fear that I was living in was the same as being that seven year old boy lying in bed with my dad paused outside the door but there was no door, there was no dad. There was truly nothing at the time for me to be afraid of and still the same fear was with me and I had no idea why I was so afraid.

My Inner Child work and Twelve Step work taught me to look at myself and see where I was wrong. I was watching myself be incredibly self-centered and selfish with no way to stop it. My mom was dying again and this time if I just did enough maybe she wouldn't leave. The problem with that plan was I wasn't doing anything.

With Val it was, if she could only *see* how much I needed her maybe she would stay.

The harder I tried the worse it got. I was in constant prayer, in continual desperation, like I was going to get caught for something and I didn't know what. Val was going to find out, the whole world was going to find out, I was a fraud. I was just one of those damn Calloway's and I wasn't ever going to amount to anything. I had spent twenty two years trying to prove them wrong and in my mind I had failed.

The accumulation of it all was more than I could shoulder. I was constantly talking about suicide and everyone who knew me was scared for me. People I didn't even know were praying for me.

It was suggested that I go see Gerald and I took the suggestion. When Gerald saw the state I was in, even he became afraid for me. While I was in Kentucky this time, I slept on his couch instead of staying with family. I felt a little bit safer there.

While in Kentucky the fear got even stronger. I could not keep an eye on Val. She might leave and I wouldn't be able to control that. I was totally aware of my need to control her and it was disgusting. I was repulsed by my own behavior.

I used sex as a measure of her investment in the relationship. On the drive back to Florida I convinced her that *we* needed to have sex as soon as I got back and made her promise me we would. We did but it was empty and very unfulfilling.

Val was done ... internally I knew it. It took a few more days (I do not remember how many) but she told me she just couldn't do it anymore and that I had to go.

I did not know what to do or where to go. "Neecy's!" The only safe place I knew to go and that was where I headed. On the way Gerald called. He was angry! I had never heard him this way. He was shouting at me telling me how selfish I was for not calling him and letting him know I had gotten back to Florida safely. He was afraid. I was crushed that he was so disappointed in me.

At Neecy's I collapsed on her couch, folded myself into the fetal position and sobbed uncontrollably. Neecy said, "Johnnie you cannot go on living like this and I cannot do it at all. I am taking you to the hospital. Now!"

I didn't argue, I just got in the car. On the way there I did say, "I think I will be okay." Neecy wasn't having it. This had been going on for over a year and was constantly getting worse. She had seen me get through many difficult times but this one frightened her. She could no longer just watch.

After almost sixteen continual years off drugs and alcohol, writing a book on spiritual principles, teaching many ACIM classes, all the rebirthings, re-enactments, literally thousands of Twelve Step meetings, totally devoting my will and my life to the God of my choosing, hundreds of hours of rehabilitation through various other means and now a mental institution? 'How?'

How the hell had I become this shell of a man, sniveling and weak with no direction and no purpose? My mind was gone. The only real thought that I could hold onto for even a minute was 'Someday, someway Johnnie you will see this as a gift.' Also, from Gerald, "This too shall pass, Son. It may be like a kidney stone but it will pass."

Some of God's gifts come in packages that are very difficult to open.

CHAPTER 20

THE OPENING

Neecy took me to the hospital ... the mental ward. I still had good insurance and they took me in.

I, Johnnie Calloway, survivor of incest, recovering alcoholic, drug addict for multiple years, the guy who survived the loss of my mother at the age of five, the kid who heard my entire childhood that I would never be anyone or amount to anything, the guy who had fallen down and gotten back up so many times that I lost count, was in a mental institution. How did this happen?

There was a lot of thought around how my mind was gone and I would never get it back. Maybe the muriatic acid had finally eaten through some nerve that disconnected parts of my mind from the part that controlled me. Maybe one of the acid trips I had taken finally took over and warped what was left of my mind. Perhaps the commercial "this is your brain on drugs" with the frying eggs was right and mine had just been simmering. I needed an answer as to why and how this could happen to me.

Maybe I was actually being punished for some great wrong I had done. Maybe God really is vengeful. Could all of my learning about an unconditionally loving God be wrong? Was this my hell?

My entire life I had looked for reason in it all. I always believed that everything and everyone had a purpose, and mine was to help others. Now in this hospital, in this nut ward, 'how was I ever going to be able to help anyone again? After all I had been through and learned, was it all for nothing? Was it all lost?' Here I stood in this place and I was absolutely helpless. None of the tools I had acquired were helping now.

In the mental ward they put me on another cocktail of drugs. They read my chart from my previous doctor and reported, "Mr. Calloway after reading your chart, it appears that you have been on all the drugs that we would want to put you on and none of them seemed to have helped. We do not know what to do with you."

Pleading with God, "Please just let me have my mind back. Please!" I spent my days wandering the rooms available to us in the ward, constantly rubbing my head and biting my lip. Periodically I would go to my room and lay in bed hugging and rocking myself, chanting, "I'm here to get better, I'm going to get better. I'm here to get better, I'm going to get better." I chanted myself to sleep most of the time and then would wake up in an absolute panic with my mind running a hundred miles an hour. "How the hell did I get here? What the hell did I do?" I would think of every little thing that I might have done to bring this on. Was this my reward for doing everything I possibly could for over twenty three years to be one of the good guys? God had truly forsaken me and I did not know why.

Visitation was on Tuesday evening and there was also a Twelve Step meeting that night. I would have so many visitors that my fellow patients often asked if I was a celebrity. My Twelve Step family came out in force. I loved that they came to see me but I was so embarrassed about my condition that I could not hold my head up and I often thought I just hadn't done a good enough job on the Twelve Steps.

Fortunately they were giving me some kind of sleep aid that worked. I hadn't truly slept in months. Just thirty minute naps throughout the night that were interrupted by waking up in a total panic and not being able to go back to sleep from the fear of waking back up.

My doctors offered the option of ECTs (Electroconvulsive Therapy), a treatment used for the severely depressed or mentally disturbed when traditional means (medications) aren't working.

I was not mentally available to help with the decision making process. It was up to Neecy, Val and Jackie. The way I understand it is they watched videos, read pamphlets and talked to the doctors. They didn't have a lot of choices because the medications weren't working, and I couldn't *live* in the hospital.

Part of the difficulty in making the decision to go ahead with the ECT was the risk of memory loss. But eventually they were in favor of the treatments… one every other day, three times a week for two weeks.

The warning turned out to be a fact. My memory was gone. My anger with Neecy and Valerie for not coming to see me the entire time I was in the hospital was intense. One or the other of them was there almost every time that was possible but I do not remember either of them ever being there.

People who had been friends for many years would visit and I would wonder why they were there because I didn't know them. The way they talked to me let me *know* I knew them, but I had no idea why or from where.

I remember having many visitors and only a few faces. My entire being was consumed by humiliation. It was just more proof that my mind was gone and actually it did not help that I had just enough mind left to know that it was gone.

Eventually the day came for them to let me out. Neither Neecy nor Val thought they could handle what was coming and their homes were not an option. I could not blame them.

My friend Tim offered me his place and I went there. I was bat-shit crazy. I could not sit still for even a few minutes. Tim was frightened. He did not know what to do with me.

While I was staying with Tim, a friend had a duct job he wanted me to help him with in Georgia. I needed the work and the money so I went. I was right back in the hell pit that I had been in before I went to the mental hospital. The trip was a disaster for me. The desperation had me panicked and my energy was very chaotic. My presence made my friend nervous and he was very concerned for me.

On the drive back from Georgia my panic level was through the roof and my driving was frightening. When we stopped for gas I asked my friend to drive for me but he would not. Even if he was driving he was afraid just to be in the truck with me.

I was on my cell phone constantly. I knew I wasn't safe and I needed help. I also knew I needed someone who would tell me the truth, even if it hurt my feelings. I called a Twelve Step Friend who was known for that ability. Tom did just what I had hoped for, "Johnnie it is not safe for you to be alone. You need to be somewhere safe. I suggest you call a homeless shelter and see if they can help."

I followed his direction and called Greg. He immediately responded, "Come in here, we will find a bed for you." It was early November of two thousand and seven, just prior to my sixteen year anniversary of abstinence from drugs and alcohol. I picked up my sixteen year sobriety medallion while living in a homeless shelter/drug and alcohol rehab.

I was quite an anomaly in the center. None of the other residents understood why someone with sixteen years clean and sober would need to be in a drug rehab and I certainly couldn't explain it.

It did not take them long to *see* why I needed help. My behavior was very erratic. I was pacing about the place and keeping to myself. I had nothing to offer the other residents and that in and of itself made me feel very small. I had been a speaker there for Twelve Step meetings many times and now I was a resident.

Humbled beyond words, I was silenced. I tried to hold on to some degree of leadership, I made sure everyone knew I had written a book, "I'm Johnnie and I wrote a book and I am sixteen years sober. I did not relapse, I just needed to be somewhere safe." That was my introduction of myself.

While at the homeless shelter they sent me to see their psychiatrist. After talking to me for about twenty minutes and reading my chart, his impression was, "Mr. Calloway my heart really goes out both to you and your previous doctors. You show symptoms of almost all the mental illnesses, ADD, ADHD, PTSD, and Bi-polar disorder. The only one I don't detect is Paranoid Schizophrenic. Your doctors have diagnosed you with each of them separately and at different times and have tried to medicate you for each. They could only diagnose the one you were showing symptoms of on the day you were with them, and I am sure it has been no picnic for you either. I am going to try to give you a medication that I believe will help with the situation in its entirety." He went on to inform me that the illness that was the strongest for me was Bi-Polar disorder. He prescribed Seroquel. I do not remember the dose but it was high. Going to sleep and staying asleep became easier and my thinking got clearer.

The Homeless Shelter made a few concessions for me. They allowed my new therapist, Eric to come see me there. After I had been there long enough to go off campus, I began to go to his office. One day in his office, sobbing profusely for about thirty minutes, I told him my tale of woe and made sure he knew about *Taming the Dragon*, teaching ACIM classes, my having almost sixteen years of continuous abstinence and all the other healing work I had accomplished; trying so hard to maintain some level of pride. He listened patiently and then looked me in the eye and said very matter of factly, "Man you are not going to like what I have to say." I responded, "That just means I probably *need* to hear it." He continued, "You do not know who God is. I do not care how many books you have written or how many ACIM classes you have taught or how long you have been abstinent. You have forgotten who God is and if you don't get Him involved in this you are going to stay fucking nuts. You cannot beat what you are up against without Him. I suggest you take your ass back to the shelter and write a letter to you from God."

That was November twenty seventh two thousand and seven. I went directly to the 'shelter' and wrote this letter:

Dear Johnnie,

I am writing you this letter because you have forgotten a few things. First, you seem to have forgotten that I love you. I love you so much. Please remember that I want only the best for you. Remember that there is NOTHING you can get yourself into that I can't get you out of. You have forgotten that I am with you always, always have been, always will be. You have confused me with a god that would punish you and therefore you have punished yourself. Please stop. Please accept all the good that I want for you into your life.

I really want you to remember how much I love you and just how important you are to Me. I need you to help my other suffering children. I have given you special gifts because I know you will use them but first you have got to allow Me to love you and to work for you. Don't let My time and effort with you be wasted. I know you won't but I'm telling you, You DON'T have to suffer anymore. It is now time for you to allow my gifts into your life.

With much Love
God

After that letter I wrote at least one letter a day for over five years, often times three or four letters a day. When the darkness would envelop me I wrote repeatedly. Just a short time after I began with the letters from God to me, I also added letters from me to God.

For a while at the 'shelter' I rode their bus to outside meetings. We had to wear name tags with the emblem on them. My recovering friends would see me with the tag and the ones that didn't know what had happened immediately assumed I was working for the shelter. Upon finding out I was a resident they then assumed I had relapsed. Very few could understand how someone, with the amount of clean time that I had, ended up there.

What was even worse was most were people I had known for years, and I didn't recognize them. My memory was still gone. They would be just jabbering away about something I had said to them that had helped them and I would be wondering, 'Who the hell are you and what in the hell are you talking about?' Since I knew that I did in fact know them I would just nod in agreement and usually say, "Aw hell." Not having a single clue as to what they were talking about.

At one of my favorite meetings where most all my male friends went, I ran into an old buddy, (Bob). He cautiously approached me and in a whisper asked, "Man, are you okay?" I tried to reassure him, "Yeah, I am fine, now."

Then he said, "The last time I saw you Johnnie, you scared the hell out of me. I really didn't know if you were still with us. I left town for a while right after I saw you and just got back. But you are okay now?" I answered, "Yeah I am okay, for the most part." He responded, "So what are you doing now? Where are you?" I told him, "I am living at a homeless shelter." He asked, "Did you relapse?", "No", I said, "It just wasn't safe for me to be alone." He volleyed, "Well we have got to get you out of there." I hesitated, "Not yet, I do not have a job or money." Quickly he came back with, "I didn't say a thing about either one of those things. I own a ten acre horse ranch with a little cottage on it that no one is living in. You can have it for free as long as you need it or as long as I own the place whichever comes first."

I immediately moved in to his cottage. I was still seeing my therapist but now he was on his own time helping me work the Twelve Steps in a way I had never done them before, with a 'Step Working Guide'.

I had done the Twelve Steps three or four times before but nothing had taken me to the depths the guide did. Almost twenty five years of involvement in the Twelve Steps and I was learning things about them I hadn't known before and using them to learn things about me that I hadn't known.

When I came out of the hospital the nightmare was not over. After the shelter it wasn't over and now at the ranch it *still* wasn't over. The ranch was a God-send and my friend was very understanding. There were nights when the fear was too much to bear and I would ask him if he would leave the door to his place open so I could sleep on his couch. He always said yes. In the mornings when I heard him stirring I would go to the cottage and back to sleep on the cottage couch.

When the terror was that strong I did not feel safe alone in the cottage and knowing someone was just in the next house wasn't enough. I still am not sure if the fear was about me hurting myself or what. I just know I could not be alone. On top of all the fear was the feeling of being so small. I was a grown fifty-year old man and afraid of the dark.

I found a new psychiatrist. He gave me a new diagnosis, 'Bi Polar II'. I had no idea what the difference was between 'Bi Polar I' and 'Bi Polar II'. 'He explained, and it went something like this: Bi Polar I is a lot like the old manic depressive term, where there are extreme highs and lows. During the high period, the patient usually feels he can conquer the world and can be very manic. With the lows they can be very depressed and often feel suicidal. With 'Bi Polar II' the lows are the same, but the high, is more of an anxiety and doesn't reach the manic level. He prescribed the same medication as the doctor I had seen at the 'shelter', but he added Lamictal. So now I was to take Lamictal and Seroquel as my new cocktail. I was terrified of new meds again. Several times my meds had been changed and every time it was a coin toss as to whether it was going to get worse or not.

I liked this doctor much more than the previous one. He actually took time to talk to me and then decided what medication to prescribe. He told me that sleep deprivation was the onset of my demise. "Johnnie, we have to get you to rest. Regular sleep will help you more than anything." He prescribed a higher dose of the Seroquel as needed to sleep. After I finally started to sleep with some regularity he lowered the dose.

I was writing my God letters constantly. I still have every one of them. Still the panic and fear were taking me down and I was immobilized with the fear of going back to the mental ward.

There were many days that I would be in the cottage screaming to my ego "Leave me the hell alone, get away from me, let me sleep, you can't win, God is with me." Often my friend would hear me and come to the cottage. I could see the concern in his eyes and once there were even tears. He would ask, "Johnnie, buddy do I need to take you somewhere? You are scaring me." I just told him, "No please trust me. I am going to beat this with God. I promise before I do anything to hurt myself I will ask you to take me somewhere." This happened many times.

I was working constantly to get better, the Twelve Steps with my former therapist now friend, constant letters to and from God, going to the gym, taking the right meds and supplements, countless hours of talking in the evening with my new Twelve Step sponsor, my Twelve Step meetings and trying to help others who were going through the hell of depression (even though I was still enmeshed in it).

With my new sponsor, George, there were many self revelations discovered that were both humbling and beneficial. With his help I learned how much of the sickness I used to manipulate people. Thank God that was not consciously. It was a tool I had learned as a child to help me cope, deeply embedded in my psyche and it was habitual. With George I learned to look at how selfish and self centered I had been. It was disgusting. But as even I had written in *Taming the Dragon*... "We must come to realize that only in facing these dragons will their fierceness diminish. In doing so, we come to know our own inner source."

I had to *see* the extent of how sick I truly was. I had known that my childhood left me with a lot of scars and they ran my life. Even after all my work I still had no idea how deep those scars went. George was helping me discover the truth and I often thought of what Ed had said in my early recovery so many years prior, "The truth shall set you free. Right after it pisses you off."

I went back to the shelter and asked if I could help others who were dealing with depression to use the Twelve Steps and to write the letters. They gladly let me lead the classes. I was still struggling but trying to help others was helping me.

Six months at the ranch and I was slowly getting better. One night I ran into an old friend in a book store. She was having a difficult time. She was sleeping in her truck. I said to her, "You can't do that anymore, come stay with me." My friend who owned the ranch understood. He let her stay with me and her company helped me immensely.

It was mid two thousand and eight and I was finally ready to go back to work. I got a job with a company that I had done business with before. I was still hanging out with Val a lot, not really sure if we were a couple or just friends. If we weren't a couple it was not due to lack of effort on my part.

Finally I could breathe again. I was sleeping, working and feeling like a human being. My memory was returning and the people coming to speak with me at my meetings I actually remembered.

A few more months at the ranch and my time was up. My friend and his life partner split up and the partner needed the cottage. I had been there a year and it had been the treatment center that I otherwise couldn't afford.

I will be forever grateful to my friend, Bob for all he did for me. He was another of God's angels sent to help me heal.

When I left the ranch it became my turn to dig in and help others.

CHAPTER 21

THE CALM

Mid January two thousand and nine, I had seventeen and a half years of abstinence from drugs and alcohol and it was time for me to leave the safe haven that God had provided me through one of his angels (Bob) and face the world. I was not upset about the departure from the ranch. I knew all along the day would have to come and somehow trusted that the right time would be shown to me. It was.

With no idea where to go or how, I did as I had so many times before, put one foot in front of the other to see where I would end up. First I went to live in George's garage. He had been there for me for countless hours of midnight counseling and now I would live in his garage.

Searching avidly for a new place, I went to the Twelve Step clubhouse, where there is a bulletin board for just such things (an affordable place). There was a note on the board that had been put there that very afternoon.

It would be a stretch … a two bed, two bath condo in Lakewood Ranch Fl. It would be *way* more than I could afford. Curiosity got the best of me (I just wanted to see it). I called the name on the note, Tom. He asked my name, "Kentucky Johnnie," my Twelve Step nickname. He said, "I do not know you but I have heard a lot of good things about you. When can you meet me there?" I answered, "Now would be fine, if you are available."

We met at the condo. It was beautiful but I knew I could not afford it. I apologized for wasting his time and said, "I simply cannot afford this." Tom said, "How do you know, I haven't said how much?" I said, "I know but I do know I can't afford this." So he asked, "What can you afford?" I figured it was worth a try, "I can afford four hundred a month if I pay utilities." Tom, without hesitation responded, "Good. It is a deal. I will be grateful for that. It will be better than getting more and then my place getting destroyed." Then it occurred to me, "Wait, I can't do first and last and there is my cat." Unfazed he said, "That's fine. When can you move in?"

I moved in around February of two thousand nine and my life was pretty normal there. I lived there for about sixteen months. I had a couple of roommates who had *great* dogs. I only had the issues any person would have for that period of time. My life was … normal?

My medications were perfect as long as I did my other work along with them. Writing the letters every day, helping others who suffered with mental illnesses or addictions, working out, going to my meetings and eating a somewhat healthy diet and I had a job I went to every day.

Val and I were still seeing each other. I stayed with her three nights a week. We weren't really a couple anymore just two really good friends with a binding history. We had gone through too much together for either of us to be able to just walk away. There were times that were difficult but what little we did still have, we wanted to keep. Even after we did break up (June of two thousand nine) and I no longer stayed with her, we still stayed close. We still went to yard sales, took care of our plants and each helped the other as much as we could.

The reason Tom had been so easy on me for the rent was the condo was in foreclosure and he wasn't paying on it so whatever he did get was just extra for him. The bank finally stepped in and I had to go.

I told Neecy that I was needing to move and she told me about a house in Bradenton Fl. And I could stay there rent free if I just took care of the place. It was perfect for me. It was like my little place that I lost to Stephanie. Finally I could have a butterfly garden again!

The backyard was my little piece of heaven. I made it my butterfly sanctuary and I built a hatching station. Butterfly caterpillars have a high number of predators ... to me that means I need to protect them. I did and do. A hatchery is a screened in box where I put the caterpillars and the plants the caterpillars need to eat. Each caterpillar has only one kind of plant they can eat, their host plant. When that plant is gone the caterpillar cannot crawl to a plant of a different variety and eat it, therefore they starve. I have made it my job to save as many as possible. So many of our butterflies are becoming extinct.

I got a job as a maintenance man at a tennis resort on Longboat Key Fl. George had told me part of my problem had been that I was only an eight- inning ballplayer. I didn't see things through to the end. That became a challenge. I should have left that job long before I did but I wanted to play the ninth inning and I did.

It had become my purpose in life to assist others battling with depression to find their way out. I have always felt that any of my experiences were just wasted time if I closed the door on it and didn't use it to help others. I taught classes at the shelter (where I used to live), the Mental Health Clinic, and spoke to kids about abuse and depression at other organizations.

It was very depressing to see how desperate the people were who came to me and how unwilling they were to do anything about it. I had created a regimen: write the letters, do the Twelve Steps (even if you weren't an addict), take your medications (many that have a mental illness will not take their medications), eat right, exercise and help others. I would often buy them the Step Guide that I had used for the steps along with the accompanying 'How and Why' book that explains the steps, a spiral notebook for the letters and another for the step work. Three different times they returned to me and said something to the effect of, 'Johnnie that is just too much work.'

I was nineteen years abstinent, been through what my friend in North Carolina called "Hell and half of Georgia" and only one guy truly wanted my help. I then decided to create a blog 'TodayILaugh.wordpress.com' (which now is 'Dragonstobutterflies.com'). I inserted many of my very personal letters to and from God on the site, daily inspirational readings, my personal journal and still most thought what I was asking of them was too much.

I wasn't asking anyone to do anything that I wasn't still doing. In my frustration my response became, "You don't want to do the work, then suffer damn it." The heart-break of walking through hell with someone and knowing there was a way out, then watching them stop just short of facing the fear that would free them was often more than I could bear.

I had my own fears going on as a result of all that had happened. Self doubt that is a part of having my diagnosis. Bi Polar II can be difficult and makes the decision making process stressful. The constant questioning, "Am I just on the high side of an episode, or is this miracle of mine real? Is what I am trying to offer these people really one of the ways out or did I just get lucky?" The doubt alone can be agonizing. I choose to believe that the route is real for me, although it may not be the way for everyone, but it is working for me.

I have always believed that everything has a reason or a purpose. I had lived through that hell so that I might be able to help others or to speak for those that can't or won't. But *no one* seemed to want my help.

Add to this all the stigmas of being Bi Polar and it was very difficult to want to continue. Especially since one of the overriding stigmas was that Bi- Polar people do not get better. Unfortunately many do not maintain their recovery from the mood swings, typically because they do not stay on their medications. I have been on the same medications for eight years now and you would have to beat me up for me to abandon them. I have, at times been a compulsive gambler but not taking my meds is one gamble I am not willing to take. I say in every class I have ever taught on the topic of depression or being Bi Polar, "The medications will never make me happy, they are only meant to stabilize my brain chemistry enough that I can do the work necessary to be happy."

For over a year I tried teaching the classes, going to the mental health services programs, helping individuals and I never felt as helpless (about helping others) as I did with these attempts. Several would approach me after the class with questions and tell me how they appreciated the class. Still, when I followed up on them, no work was being done.

As Ed had said so many years prior, "The truth shall set you free, right after it pisses you off." I have since added, " ... or breaks your heart.

Some use our sickness to justify their behavior. Not all, but some. I am definitely one that did. For me facing that truth was one of the most difficult things I had ever done for my betterment. Yes, the abuses of my childhood, the loss of my mother, the multiple addictions, the stigma of being in a small town with a "bad bunch" reputation, were all *used* to justify my doing what I wanted when I wanted. "After all", I would rationalize, "with what I have gone through, who could blame me?"

One guy, Bobby, made the work worthwhile. He did everything I asked him to do and more. We had a mutual friend, Jack who directed him to me. Jack had witnessed my miracle and had seen me up close and personal when I was at my worst. He had also witnessed the turn around. He knew I had 'been there, done that', and he thought I could help Bobby.

Bobby came to me before the elevator had gotten to the basement with him and with his willingness to do the work, he got results very quickly.

I am not proud to say this but one in one hundred and fifty was not enough to keep me doing all the work.

In the latter part of two thousand eleven I partnered with a Twelve Step friend in an air conditioning company. That lasted almost to the end of two thousand thirteen. I had pretty much given up on saving the planet and decided finally to just be a spoke in the wheel instead of the trying to be the hub.

In October two thousand thirteen, I moved out of the little house in Bradenton and into, a fifty-five and older mobile home park. I live there still today.

In December of two thousand fourteen I installed an air conditioner in a rental unit in Tri Par and I met Suzi, the tenant. While working there I told her about my butterfly garden and *Taming the Dragon*. She visited the garden and read the book. She fell in love with both. At our community pool she shared about my garden and my book with Ruth who also visited my garden and read my book. She definitely fell in love with the butterflies and enjoyed the book as well. Ruth so happens to sit on the board of directors for a foundation which was developed as a result of a book written by another author, Chip St. Clair. He had also written about his childhood of abuse.

Ruth shared his book with Suzi who could not wait to share it with me. I am very picky about what I read. If a book doesn't catch me in the first couple of pages it is over. This book, *The Butterfly Garden* got me in the preface. I started reading on a Tuesday around five p.m. and was finished by Thursday around ten p.m.

During the entire time of reading, my thoughts were, 'This guy grew up in my house.' I felt a kinship with the writer and I wished I had his courage. He was living *my* dream. He had created his Foundation and was helping at-risk children through their various programs in the schools. I wanted to play with them.

Ruth had to go up north for business and while there she shared a copy of *Taming the Dragon* with her author friend, Chip ... the only copy I had. When she returned home she had left the book behind. I was upset. My thoughts were, 'I have no real education, I was told my entire childhood that I would not amount to anything and I wrote a damn book and now I have no proof of that fact.'

The publisher of *Taming the Dragon* had taken off and left his other authors with nothing. In my case I no longer even had my pdf. Getting it printed again was going to cost more money than I had. In short, in my mind, it was gone. A week later Chip and his wife, Lisa came to Sarasota, with my book. They had no idea what my not having it meant to me.

When they got here I requested a meeting with him and he agreed. I wanted to pick his brain about his horrendous childhood. While sitting with him our connection was strong. He told me he loved *Taming the Dragon* and that I was a very talented writer. And … he said, "You have a gift and you have a story, tell it." … the permission I needed!

Taming the Dragon and *Dragons to Butterflies* are two entirely different styles of writing. I didn't think I could write the facts. The first book was/is a metaphor of my life. *Dragons to Butterflies* is about the facts of my life.

A couple of days after my meeting with Chip I began writing *Dragons to Butterflies*. Once I started I could not stop. I was up writing until three or four in the morning. To write in detail the events of my life as vividly as I have attempted to do here, I *had* to go there. Some of it was excruciatingly painful, some of it was incredibly joyful. I was already having breakfast with Ed every morning and when I began writing he indulged me by reading what I had written the night before. Reliving the pain and torment sent me back to weekly meetings with Callie. The pain, the confusion, the losses and the love were real and often terrifying. But … I had to write it!

I have no idea where my life goes from here. But as a result of this book I now know without a doubt that I am meant to help others.

Often times in the last few chapters of this book, I asked myself, 'Where is the happy ending? You don't have the big house, the nice car, the loving devoted wife or the big bank account.' Fortunately my friends have helped me with the happy ending because to a great degree, my friends *are* my happy ending.

Four in the morning a week ago, I remembered a quote from one of Richard Bach's books,

"I gave my life to become the person I am right now. Was it worth it?"

My answer:

Hell Yes!

I just do not want to do it again.
A new journey begins ...

CHAPTER 22

WHAT IF?

In the previous twenty one chapters I shared the story of my life. To break away and tell how the lessons fit in would have taken away from the story. Now I will share how I found my way through it all.

As the story would have it, I am not just a human being here trying to have a spiritual experience, I am a spiritual being here having a human experience. That really sounds nice but what exactly does it mean? I am, as a spiritual being not confined to a body, a personality, my personal story or the judgments of my surroundings. God created us in His image and His likeness; therefore we are not powerless if we are connected to Him.

For me, as in all things that I share here, this is *my* truth and is in no way meant to suggest what someone else should believe. These teachings are what I have used to find my way through the dark.

ACIM: Text PP. 448
"I am responsible for what I see
I choose the feelings I experience, and I decide
Upon the goal I would achieve.
And everything that seems to happen to me
I ask for and receive as I have asked."

220

The first time I read this my mind raced and yet it comforted me. 'I asked for my mom to die? No way!' But if we are truly spiritual beings here having a human experience and if life is seen as a classroom, could it be that I asked for the *lesson* that would come from her death? For me that explained the random acts of insanity that had occurred in my life and opened the door for me to have a better understanding and faith in an Unconditionally Loving God. Nothing happens to me but everything happens for me. "If" the responsibility statement mentioned above is true and I believe it is, then the things I've seen I have chosen to see. The feelings felt, I chose to feel. My seeming failures have not been failings at all! I have achieved the goals I chose to achieve. And all of it has been a result of my asking. This concept can be very difficult to wrap our minds around. And even for a long time student of ACIM, very confusing.

I, Johnnie Calloway, this physical body, did not consciously sit and decide for any of the details that made up my life. I did not come out of my mother's womb and say, "Okay I am here to learn. Let's get the party started and we can begin with twenty eight seizures." I, Johnnie Calloway did not decide that my mother should die, that my father should be the ogre that he was in my family, to be a drug addict/alcoholic or to have so many mental and emotional issues. I do believe however, that the part of me that is a part of God did choose/ask to come here and learn on as deep a level as possible the principle of forgiveness both for self and others and hopefully and ultimately discover that to forgive myself is forgiving others and vice versa. My life was/is not a collection of random acts of insanity. "To me," means I was a victim. "For me," means that everything that has occurred in my life, if I allow myself to see it that way, has been there to serve the ultimate purpose

221

and goal of forgiveness, which my soul desired. It has therefore been "for me."

What "if" I chose not to follow the world's curriculum? What "if" my spirit self had only one goal in mind and that goal was/is forgiveness and love of self and others, and to learn the difference between what is valuable and what is valueless? The ego's "prizes" in life aren't the true prizes. I am actually very wealthy with the true prizes.

I am not saying there is anything wrong with those prizes, I am saying that if I had those prizes and not the others, I am still wanting and nothing will ever be enough.

With the responsibility concept I am no longer a victim to a vengeful and angry Creator but I am co-creator in my life. Also "if" I have created or helped create the mess in my life, "if" I do have that power then I also have the power to at least help undo it. This at least somewhat explains the age old question "Why do bad things happen to good people?" When I accept the responsibility statement, I know hope and I feel empowered.

This all seems to be a big stretch, but remember, Ed had told me way back in the beginning of my turn around, "It might behoove you to be open to the idea that perhaps everything you think you know about God could be wrong." I have since come to believe that is not only about God but life in general and it is important for me to daily hold on to that possibility. Open-mindedness embodies the idea that maybe I am wrong and without an open mind I cannot learn and grow.

My Lessons

First and foremost, as lessons go, there is my momma. She is where it all began and possibly where it will end. She was, even in her physical absence, a spiritual inspiration for me my entire life. My wanting to please her and make her proud has been my guide even during the times when that desire was not tangible. Her passing and my guilt over it has taught me about the uselessness of guilt and the incredible power of love. Guilt became a habit for me, a way of life. With the guilt I carried over her death, I am still learning self forgiveness. Her death has been one of my greatest, lessons and gifts. It has made me use all the tools and therefore made her one of my greatest teachers.

Through my dad I learned the importance of forgiveness. Through ACIM I learned how to truly forgive, not just give it lip service. My sameness with my dad? ACIM states "Your true healing lies in identifying with your sameness." With my Twelve Step work I found the honesty that would allow me to *see* how my dad and I were alike. The mistake that I made with this part of the process was/is trying to identify with the exact form of any wrongdoing. My argument for a very long time, "I would never do to a child the things my dad had done to my loved ones and myself. I would never sexually molest a young child or beat an old woman." But I trusted the book, *A Course in Miracles*, so I dug deeper for the answer. It was true I wouldn't do those things in the same way (form) that he did but there were other ways that I disempowered and harmed people.

How else was I like my father? Like him I wanted more than anything to be loved and had no idea as to how to trust it and therefore was terrified of it. I would do anything to acquire it and then do everything I could to prove I didn't deserve it. I (we) sought for proof that it wasn't real and wouldn't last. This is also the common bond of all human beings.

In following this line of thinking I discovered the *real* gift; my dad is my spiritual brother.

Through my Twelve Step and ACIM training I had discovered, "I do not see what I look *at* but rather what I look *for*." If I am looking for reasons someone cannot be trusted, I will find them. I learned of the part of my mind that wants me dead and will settle for unhappy. My ego would have me do anything to disconnect me from God and my fellow man.

The miracle of all Twelve Step programs is unity, identification and fellowship. What if the unity, identification and fellowship were carried outside those rooms and into the world at large? What if those rooms are only a beginning for all to become unified through identification and fellowship? What if all the gatherings, classes, and meetings where we join in our separate pods and speak of unity became one pod? What if in truth there is only one pod anyway? In the meetings we speak of 'identification not comparison'. Think of what it would be like if we did that everywhere.

What *if* all the dragons in my life were butterflies all along?

What *if* I'm not the only one it would benefit to be open to the idea of being wrong?

As far as the happy ending:

My happy ending is as much about whom and what I am not, as it is about who and what I am. I am not drunk, high, in jail, in a mental institution or living in the streets. I am a good friend, a good brother (I hope my sisters will agree with that) and a good person.

What writing *Dragons to Butterflies* has done for me is to give me the opportunity to remember things both good and bad that were long since forgotten. It has been a process rich with life and emotion.

Some of the personal revelations have been somewhat difficult to embrace. I have realized that a lot of the inner work that I have done has had an ego driven goal attached to it, the prize or reward at the end (the girl, the nice house, the car and/ or the fat bank account). Some of the free giving wasn't so free. I wasn't necessarily looking for a return gift from the recipient of my gifts but I *was* looking for it from God. Time after time I tried to do the big things to help others but ... Mary Padlak had told me in my very first session with her that money would never happen for me until I wrote. I wrote *Taming the Dragon* and I was still broke. I wanted to believe that *Taming the Dragon* would help people and that was why I wrote it. The truth is I did/do want to help but I also wanted/want the prize. When my hopes weren't realized, resentment became my prize but I got up and tried again.

My relationship with God has been much like my relationships with my mom and women in general. 'If I just do enough, if I am just good enough, maybe then He will reward me.' They never came or they came and I wasn't able to hold onto them. On some very deep level I blamed God. Very deep in my soul I have held onto the idea that He has punished me. On a more conscious level I have forgiven Him but that wounded child that lives within me (that can at times run my life) still believes God has punished me.

All this time I have hoped for a God Who would reward me at the end of all my endeavors. Today I do not think it is possible to believe in a God that would reward and not believe in a God that would/will punish.

My God does not punish me but *I* do and *I* have. I believe today that my "failings" have been largely due to my addiction to guilt, fear and self sabotage and the possibility that I still have not truly forgiven myself for my mother's death and all the things that were its result. I held on to and used that guilt to justify my actions for so long as a child, that it became the deepest habit of my life.

My ego has been vigilant about its pursuit of my *not* knowing peace. I must now be vigilant about my pursuit of peace and stay aware that my peace will not be the result of acquiring the prize at the end but that *peace is* the prize.

Also in the process of writing *Dragons to Butterflies*, I was sharing chapter by chapter with a handful of trusted friends and they would ask questions that helped me fill in the missing pieces. The most important question was, "Why are you writing this?" The first time I was asked this question I was actually startled. Grasping for an answer I responded with, "I hope it might help some people." That was not the truth. That has become the truth but it wasn't so in the beginning. The real truth was, writing *Dragons to Butterflies* was just the next thing to do. When I was told, "You need to write the real story" I only started writing because it was next in my life and once I started, it took on a life all its own. I simply could not stop. I started the process on February eighteenth and the outline was finished May the fourth. As I am writing the end of the revisions it is now May the sixteenth.

And ... on May the eighteenth the real gift of *Dragons to Butterflies* came for me. I forgot to take my medications and could not fall to sleep. Not knowing I had forgotten, I started trying all the falling asleep tricks I've acquired over the years and nothing was working. I began to breathe as I had been taught in rebirthing classes and suddenly ... I was lying in that hospital bed with my mom. I thought, 'Why am I here? I've done this already.' But then my granddad, Clifford appeared and he had a demeanor about him that I had never seen; he was soft, caring and compassionate but the most interesting of all ... he was frightened! In this vision he embraced me and my mom and my heart softened for him. In this vision he became human and I forgave the one person who in all my life I had withheld forgiveness from. In that moment I took three giant steps forward to the self forgiveness that I have withheld from myself.

Self forgiveness is the gift that I hope to give myself as a result of *Dragons to Butterflies*.

I would be lying if I said that now that it is written there isn't a part of me (a big part) that still wants the prize … yes, the girl, the car, the home and the fat bank account. There are debts that I owe to people that have loved me and I them. I hope my next expression of self love is for those debts to be paid.

If this helps someone to find self forgiveness that will make it worthwhile. I truly feel that God wanted me to write this down. I will play the ninth inning here but I have no idea where it will lead. I am as eager as anyone to see where I go next.

I like being Johnnie Calloway today. I may not love myself as much as I could but I no longer hate myself. And that in itself is miracle and a huge prize.

I guess I am supposed to say "The End" but it is not the end. A new journey awaits me I am sure. Staying true to my playful nature, I'll simply say,

"What *if*...there is no end?

I encourage you to visit my website DragonsToButterflies. com for daily affirmations, letters to God and a place to share your comments, questions and experiences.

EPILOGUE

Let's be clear, the title *Dragons to Butterflies* may be a little misleading. I am no butterfly. A butterfly is a completed work of art. I am not complete. I raise butterflies and build butterfly gardens today. It is one of my true passions. I have done so in varying degrees for fifteen years. I love the butterfly. Butterfly gardening and butterflies are my safe place today. They are my new closet but it is beautiful, bright and warm in here. Whenever I watch a butterfly it reminds me to thank God for the many gifts, blessings, teachers and lessons in my life.

Over the years I have had the privilege of watching and studying every phase of the butterfly's life; the egg, the microscopic caterpillar, the adult "cat," the process of the "cat" becoming a chrysalis and the emergence of the butterfly from the chrysalis. The magic, the miracle and the mystery of the butterfly is what goes on inside the chrysalis. The metamorphosis, as I see it, symbolizes the transformation in our lives.

My metamorphosis has been at times incredibly beautiful and excruciatingly painful but always full of life and passion.

There were other teachers, gifts, lessons and tools used in the process of my transformation, too many to include them all in this book. They will be disclosed in my next work:

<u>Within the Chrysalis</u> - *<u>It's an Inside Job</u>*
Thank You

Johnnie Calloway

CPSIA information can be obtained at www.ICGtesting.com
Printed in the USA
LVOW07s0620050416

482146LV00001B/1/P